SCHOOL IMPROVEMENT:

Revitalize Your School with Strategic Planning

SCHOOL IMPROVEMENT:
Revitalize Your School with Strategic Planning

Dr. Debra A. Tracy

This book was printed in the United States of America.

To order additional copies of this book, contact:
Xlibris Corporation
1-888-795-4274
www.Xlibris.com
Orders@Xlibris.com
105255

CONTENTS

INTRODUCTION

The demands placed on principals have continued to increase in today's educational climate. In addition to the traditional role, principals must be concerned with school improvement and accountability by meeting improvement goals as well as reaching standards. But in the day-to-day operation of a school, strategic planning is far from the minds of most principals. Think about the number of details a principal must consider daily. The list is long and involved and covers a wide range of topics. When I was a building principal, I found out firsthand that the number of issues that arise and decisions that need to be made can be overwhelming. Even as a well-planned and organized principal, thoughts raced through my mind constantly. The first thoughts early in the morning seemed to begin with the structure and organization of the day. Prior to arriving at the building each day, I was concerned about staffing and thought about teacher absences, wondering whether or not vacancies would be filled with substitute teachers. From there on, there were busy days contemplating issues, such as safety and security, parent concerns, teacher questions, student behavior, and discipline, to name a few. From the arrival of the buses in the morning to the end of the last event of the day, numerous issues were addressed and decisions were made at a moment's notice. Down to the smallest decisions that are made, principals are held accountable on many levels.

All of the daily administrative decisions relate to the ultimate goal of student achievement, either directly or indirectly. Therefore, from the way classes are scheduled to the way you greet students each day, the culture and climate are being set with each decision. The decisions that you make influence the direction in which you guide the school as well as student achievement. Others notice how you handle daily decision making because your approach in handling decisions demonstrates what is important. Your decisions must convey the message that student achievement is of the utmost importance. If your decisions are not aligned with the goals or with the priorities you maintain, others will see that as operating inconsistently. When viewed as having inconsistencies between your stated beliefs and your actions, the staff and others within the school community will be less likely to trust in your leadership. Dually important in leadership are the tasks of setting the goals as well as how you approach those goals. Effective principals understand that decisions made each day impact the school's climate. When the day-to-day decisions mirror your goals, you will gain the trust, respect, and support that are necessary in the strategic planning efforts. You will be able to build a culture of trust and respect throughout your school, which is vital to good leadership.

Successful principals have the desire to improve their schools and the learning opportunities for students. The best way to accomplish this is by means of a well-planned process. The problem is that most principals have not been formally instructed on how to make this happen. Each principal has his or her own way of approaching this important responsibility; nonetheless, improvement is most often accomplished through trial and error. Even the best and most experienced principals struggle to bring about significant improvements, particularly in low-performing schools. You may have innovative ideas to implement or the staff may be trying to incorporate the best research-based strategies, but unless the efforts are set into an organized, overall plan for your building, you cannot be sure of what will happen. The school will find itself at year's end, hoping that the test scores have improved. You cannot risk the "wait and see" approach. You need to know along the way that progress is being made toward your goals in order to realize measurable gains.

No matter what type of educational setting is involved, each has a unique set of issues and circumstances to manage on a daily basis that are not only time consuming but also seemingly urgent. You can be weighed down with the daily tedium that controls you rather than you being able to control it. That is not to say you won't have problems to handle; you will, however, be able to minimize the crises that do arise throughout each day and maximize the time you have to handle the most important issues. Imagine a solution to managing it all. The solution is strategic planning.

The strategic planning process is one of the most important ventures you can undertake as a building principal. This is especially true for buildings that fail to meet adequate yearly progress (AYP), according to federal guidelines. Failing to meet federal standards is an essential reason to tackle an improvement process, which you may be facing. However, improvement, restructuring, reform, transformation, or revitalization of schools is best accomplished when the school sees the need and works together at the individual building level to make improvements, not when it is forced upon you based on district, state, or national mandates. The impetus for transformation must be the school's desire to improve learning outcomes for students. In other words, you must take charge of making improvements because it is important and it is the right thing to do. Don't wait until you are faced with an "improve or else" scenario. It is in the best interest of the school to institute an improvement process before it becomes mandatory and, perhaps, even out of your hands. Through building a unified plan created by the building leadership and those responsible for its implementation, you will demonstrate that student outcomes and achievement are important. The school will have the direction and focus necessary to reach the desired goals.

Entering into the improvement process will most assuredly involve scrutinizing every aspect of the school, which may, at times, prove to be uncomfortable for some. Most people do not want to hear that the work they have been doing has not produced the desired results, yet many are averse to changing their practices. Understand that change is never easy, particularly when discussing a topic such as strategic planning, but change is necessary for improvement and growth. In schools where teaching and learning are meaningful and engaging, educators continually assess the quality of their efforts and continually focus on improving their instruction and, in turn, student outcomes. The strategic planning process is a focused and clear process for leading change. It will help you to clarify the school's priorities and will result in the establishment of a clear path to reach your vision. Credibility as a leader will be gained, a sense of trust among the staff will be established, and cohesiveness will be built within your team. Strategic planning is a process that must be owned by your staff. Collaboration is required in the development of the plan. By allowing everyone to be a part of the process, you can be sure that the total school community will be more likely to work enthusiastically to support it. You may even encounter unintended results in the course of creating and implementing your plan. Unintended results can be beneficial to the overall atmosphere of the building. In other words, while you set out to improve achievement, you may produce improvement in other areas, such as communication, collaboration, school-community relations, or resource management.

This book was written as a guide for school principals and school leadership teams who are on the mission of school improvement. It has been created for the purpose of assisting individual building level teams with the process of school improvement through strategic planning. Strategic planning is not the latest fad or the next best program that will come and go but is a process that will stand the test of time. It is the tool that can assist you, the staff, and the school in truly taking on the task of reorganization and improvement, or what I like to call revitalization of your school based on the goals you create and the process you establish. In this book, you will learn how to create and implement a meaningful strategic plan that will move your school toward success.

Every school building is different; therefore, as you prepare to tackle this important work, the school community must be willing to incorporate its own values and beliefs into this process. It is vital that these are reflected in the plan to maintain a sense of community and ownership. Simply stating that you are implementing a strategic plan does not guarantee success or desired results. As a matter of fact, some research even supports the notion that strategic planning may be ineffective. The difference between an effective plan and an ineffective plan is the manner in which the strategies are generated and in the manner in which the process is executed while following the prescribed steps. Building a successful plan takes a commitment by all members in the organization.

The current climate in education is that of continuous change. To list a few examples, right now in the state of Ohio, discussion regarding revising and increasing standards for students is taking place. One urban district in particular is in the process of looking for new programs that will assist them with improving reading achievement. A great number of schools are continuing to post large gaps in achievement between various demographic groups. For instance, gaps exist between low socioeconomic and high socioeconomic students and between racial groups. More students than ever are taking remedial courses when they enter college. These topics point to the fact that current practices are not working to meet the needs of all of our students. Schools are continuing to struggle to bring about the desired improvements.

Even if you are working in a high-performing school, how do you know you are meeting the needs of all of your students? While the overall performance of the building may be excellent, there are likely a number of students who are falling below the standards who need assistance to be successful. Maybe you have tried a variety of programs that all but guaranteed results only to find that they did not work in your school. Perhaps you have let teachers try their own strategies, hoping that their ideas would make a difference. For all of these reasons, instead of continuing to try different ideas or guess at what might work, you need a well-thought-out, reliable plan to make a difference. Strategic planning can stimulate improvement and put you on a track to success. The strategic planning model will be an invaluable blueprint for growth and revitalization of your school. Although not a quick fix, strategic planning can be a systematic, organized, and efficient approach to generating impressive results. You will find out that you already possess the necessary components you need to get started. What it takes is putting it all together in a planned, meaningful process to get results. You can do it with the assistance of this strategic planning model.

Chapter Overviews

Chapter 1 introduces the concept of strategic planning while providing definitions for terms used in the process. Strategic planning in education evolved from business models and became broadly accepted in the late 1980s and the early 1990s. A theoretical connection to the Pygmalion effect and the attribution theory is made regarding their relevance to the process. The value that the strategic planning process plays in school improvement involves key areas, such as accountability, collaboration, and defining a direction for the school. The six phases of the strategic planning process are presented. The chapter concludes with a discussion of time management and an activity to use with teachers during a professional development session to illustrate the benefits of good time management.

Chapter 2 takes a look at the strategic planning process as a school improvement model. As you prepare to begin the process, a timeline should be set as a guide. Planning for the process is as important as the process itself, and selecting staff to serve on the planning team requires thoughtful consideration. This chapter details several options for selecting members of the team and recommends the best approach. While this book is generally for use by building principals and building leadership, strategies for district improvement teams are also provided. A goal-based approach and an issue-based approach to improvement are described and recommended for certain situations. The steps in the strategic planning process are identifying the purpose, mission, vision, and goals; collecting and analyzing data; writing the plan; implementing the plan; monitoring and evaluating progress; and revising the plan.

Chapter 3 details the very important stages of developing your purpose, mission, vision, and goals for the strategic planning process in your building. Even though most schools may have mission and vision statements, it is important to review and perhaps revise them when beginning this process. A group process for creating the purpose, mission, and vision statements is presented. When developing goals for your plan, creating SMART goals will ensure your plan starts out on solid ground. A model for developing SMART goals, along with several examples, is included. Communication in this, as well as all other phases of the process, is extremely important to maintain.

Chapter 4 discusses data collection and data analysis related to decision making. As you think about the improvements you want to make in your building, you should aim to support your decisions with data that show where improvements need to be made. When it's time to determine whether or not improvements have been made, you will have a starting point from which to compare results from one time period to the next. Data can be gathered from a variety of areas and can be derived from both quantitative and qualitative sources. The analysis of your data will identify the areas for improvement as well as the extent to which improvements need to occur. Gap analysis, frequency distribution, and item analysis are discussed.

Chapter 5 examines the writing phase of the process. Utilizing a school planning team (SPT), the goals will be written then shared with the school community. A planning template is presented, along with examples of goals, strategies, and action steps. Strategies and action steps will be developed for each of the goals in the planning document. The action plan format is introduced along with examples of how to complete each section. Key points for communicating the plan are reviewed.

Chapter 6 considers the implementation of the plan by looking at the process from the perspective of an administrator, teacher, student, and school community member. Communication remains a critical piece in the implementation phase. Keys to successful implementation such as leadership, commitment, belief in the plan, and praise and recognition are presented. The reasons plans often fail are discussed which include lack of input, lack of definition, lack of clarity, lack of detail, lack of interest, and lack of monitoring.

Chapter 7 presents monitoring and evaluation practices necessary for determining the success of your plan. Monitoring and evaluation are explained along with purposes and uses for each. Monitoring is an ongoing process that requires a great deal of attention by those responsible for overseeing the implementation. Some of the benefits of monitoring the strategic planning process are to inform decision making, convey the importance of the plan, inspire continued improvement, ensure results are being met, enable adjustments to be made along the way, and provide critical information for the evaluation process. Evaluation techniques will vary based on individual school needs. The benefits of evaluating the strategic plan are to determine whether or not your strategies were successful, identify whether or not the goals were appropriate, document results, provide comparison data, present a true picture of the school, and deliver accountability. A status report is a tool for teachers to use to track and monitor progress of their students on a regular basis. A sample of this report is presented.

Chapter 8 deals with revising the strategic plan. This phase is the most subjective of the six phases because the revisions will be based on the results for your individual building or setting. The need for changes to the plan typically arises for one of three reasons: changes in the external environment, changes in "client" needs, or perceived ineffectiveness of the current plan. If goals are not being met, there may be a need for changes in the implementation of the plan or there may be a need for changes in the plan itself. Assistance needs to be provided for teachers who are experiencing difficulty with implementation of their responsibilities within the action plans.

Any school that is committed to improvement will find value from the information presented in this book. As the principal, you can lead the charge in making the changes necessary to improve your school. You cannot do it alone, nor will it be easy. By revitalizing your staff and creating a committed team of educators, positive changes will occur that can result in dramatic improvements in student outcomes.

Revitalizing your school connotes a reawakening or a fresh, new beginning for your building, your staff, and your students. That is exactly what you can generate by utilizing this process. It becomes necessary to utilize this approach when you see that your academic achievement results not moving in the direction or are not moving as quickly as you desire. As you will discover, you already have the elements necessary to make school improvement a reality. This process does not require any special program or product, but relies on your commitment and leadership to inspire positive changes. Working collaboratively with all areas of the school community on this process, you will be able to accomplish the type of results you wish to achieve.

CHAPTER 1

The Importance of Strategic Planning

Without strategic planning, the daily role of a building principal falls into that of a reactionary. Crisis management becomes the norm to principals who do not plan because time is spent on reacting to events that occur during the day rather than on setting a clear path for what should take place. How can strategic planning assist in managing crises? Imagine beginning the day without any idea of what you want to accomplish. You spend your time jumping from one activity to the next, from one situation to another, and at the end of the day you ask yourself what has been accomplished. You know that there is still much work that needs to be done with responsibilities, such as planning for a staff meeting, handling paperwork, or returning telephone or email messages before your day ends. Conversely, with a strategic plan in place you will set the expectations and have routines and procedures in place to address daily concerns. Crises will be minimized because good planning will, first, prevent many incidents from happening, and second, prepare everyone to handle those that do occur.

While organization is an entirely different topic to master, suffice it to say that if you are lacking in organizational skills, you can spend an enormous amount of time on tasks and activities that detract from your mission. As the principal, you should not be the person who handles all of the issues or crises throughout the day. Others can be charged with some of these responsibilities, provided that sufficient processes are in place to handle them. Strategic planning can be the vehicle for delegating responsibilities to others in the school so that you can focus on essential matters, most importantly, instructional leadership, while still being able to complete your tasks working smarter, not harder or longer. Although issues and crises cannot be ignored, they are less likely to materialize when the direction is clearly developed and a strategic plan incorporating detailed action steps is in place. In addition, with strategic planning, the number of incidents that occur each day will be reduced because of your planning and organization. With better structure and planning that is aligned with the mission, you will have a smoothly run operation where everyone is aware of what to do when certain situations arise.

Most school districts operate with some type of process to guide their improvement goals. Beyond that, individual buildings within a district will benefit from following this strategic planning process to develop an individual building plan. Where a district improvement plan already exists, creating your building plan may be somewhat easier and less time consuming due to the fact that the goals and possibly some strategies are already spelled out in the district plan. The individual building plan will reflect the district goals and strategies but will be a much more detailed and comprehensive document. Many schools have instituted improvement plans in response to state and federal mandates and calls for accountability. While schools generally take part in some form of a planning process, many of these processes are not as complete or as far-reaching as the process set forth in this book. A comprehensive process, such as the one presented here, is essential for improving achievement and getting the results you desire for your students and your school. The manner in which the school operates in terms of working toward the goals must be evident to and understood by everyone. Consequently, successful schools operate with a plan to continuously work toward meeting the vision and goals while following a roadmap to reach their destination.

Over a number of years, business practices, such as strategic planning, have been adapted for use in educational organizations.

Although strategic planning has been active in the business world for many decades, it was popularized and became broadly accepted in educational organizations many years later during the late 1980s and the early 1990s. While strategic planning has been discussed and practiced in education for over twenty years, limited information exists regarding a specific process to follow for the implementation of a strategic plan. This is the only model of its kind created for use as an improvement model in educational organizations.

Despite the fact that strategic planning was adapted from the business setting, educators must have their own manner of executing the process. The writings of Henry Mintzberg maintain that planning in business organizations does not necessarily translate to good planning in education. He contends that the process for use in educational organizations is lacking because it does not explain how to formulate good organizational strategy. Most literature on the subject of strategic planning in education includes information regarding the phases in the process, data collection, evaluation strategies, and implementation of the strategies. The major drawback, however, is that the literature does not discuss how to create good strategy in the first place. The planning tool presented in this book emphasizes a sound process for thinking and acting strategically along with how to create good strategy. Both of which are essential to the process. What you will find in this book is a complete and explicit model intended for principals to follow in pursuit of school improvement.

Long-Range Planning versus Strategic Planning

Historically referred to as long-range planning in business applications, strategic planning in education differs in a number of important ways. The following table illustrates several of the main differences between long-range planning and strategic planning.

Dr. Debra A. Tracy

Long-Range Planning vs. Strategic Planning

	Long-Range Planning	Strategic Planning
Methodology	Primarily quantitative	Primarily qualitative
Data source	Numbers driven	Idea driven
Basis	Projection	Vision
Mind-set	Inside out	Outside in
Environment	Stable	Changing
Focus	Final blueprint	Planning process

Figure 1.1. Differences between long-range planning and strategic planning.

Long-range planning represents a straightforward approach that tends to remain the same throughout the entire process where the results are examined at the end. It operates on the assumption that a stable environment is present during the implementation of the plan and will remain so to reach the goals. In addition, long-range planning is more likely to deal with quantitative data and utilizes past data to make predictions or set goals for the future. While strategic planning does rely on quantitative data to demonstrate growth, qualitative data are utilized throughout the process to ascertain information regarding the needs of the organization and how well the process is proceeding. It is a process that can respond to the ever changing environment in education. A strategic plan is, in a sense, a living document that can be modified when new information arises or when the circumstances become altered. Strategic planning is sufficiently fluid to allow the planning team to reflect on the progress and make adjustments at predetermined stages of the process. At the same time, strategic planning is designed in such a manner as to maintain its structure by following the established steps. The long-range planning process takes the current state of the organization then projects what it will do in the future. Conversely, the strategic planning process sets a vision for the future and identifies how it will get there. Strategic planning looks at the nature of the problems and the potential of the organization to identify appropriate strategies and then responds to the needs in order to meet its goals.

Definitions

The array of definitions for "strategic planning" ranges from short, simple statements that contain minimal detail, such as a focus on objectives and goals, to complex and detailed definition that includes a description, such as a vision, goals, objectives, and the organization's direction or a tactical plan to achieve desired goals. Most definitions describe the process as a means of determining an organization's long-term goals and then identifying the most appropriate approach to achieve those goals. As you work through the process of strategic planning, you will encounter various terms that will apply to the document as well as to the process itself. The following list of terms will be used in the explanation of this planning tool. The terms described here are offered as operational definitions related to this strategic planning tool and are applicable to the process in the educational environment.

Strategic Planning: The process of identifying the organization's needs and objectives then developing strategies and action plans to meet the stated needs and objectives. Everyone works toward the same goals. Strategic planning provides the framework and serves as the roadmap for the organization and for all decisions that are made.

Process: A set of actions performed in a specific manner in order to reach a desired goal or outcome.

Mission: A concise statement about the work of the organization, the objectives, and the reasons the organization exists. It is the overall expression of the purpose of the organization that includes who we are, what we aim to achieve, and how we aim to achieve it. The mission helps clarify the work that is performed.

Vision: A statement of purpose in terms of values and what the organization wants to be in the future. The statement reflects the ideal state the organization wishes to become.

Goals: The organization's goals are stated in broad terms and indicate what the organization wishes to achieve in the long term.

Strategy: A statement of action that guides an organization toward its desired future. The strategy is the overall approach or method to address a particular need. It does not spell out specific activities but describes what you want to do to achieve a goal.

Data-driven decision making: Using assessment results or other information that is gathered about students or the school to make decisions related to goal setting or planning.

Gap Analysis: The organization must analyze the difference between its current state and its desired future state in all areas. The difference is called the gap. In analyzing the gap, you need to determine the reasons for the gaps and then find ways to address the difference. Gap analysis may also refer to comparing data from various demographic groups (for example, socioeconomic groups or gender).

Initiatives: Initiatives are particular district or school ideas that will be incorporated into the strategic plan and implemented throughout the duration of the plan. Initiatives may be programs purchased through outside vendors or may be programs or processes developed in-house.

Action Plan: A set of strategies or tasks the organization will undertake in order to reach its goals. The action plan contains the indicators used to measure success and contains strategies, how the strategies will be implemented, who is responsible for making sure the strategies are implemented or who is implementing the strategies, resources needed, evidence of success, and a timeline for completion.

Action Step: An individual objective or unit within the action plan that defines how the strategy will be implemented to achieve the goals. There can be multiple action steps for a given strategy.

Status Report: A document that is used by classroom teachers to monitor student progress on a monthly or quarterly basis. The report includes general demographic information about each student as well as areas such as past achievement information, current levels of performance, engagement, and effort.

Theory into Practice

A strategic plan must be viewed as a tool used to improve student achievement and not simply as a task to be completed and placed on a shelf. The process involves determining what the organization wants to do and how it will do it, where the organization wants to go and how it will get there, and perhaps most importantly, how it will know if it got there or not. Strategic planning, if properly planned and carried out, can be the vehicle for assisting your school in achieving the goals established at the beginning of the process. Results will be achieved with the proper mind-set of the leadership and everyone involved with the organization.

A study conducted by Douglas Reeves and Stephen White that was reported in *Educational Leadership* (2007/2008) noted the impact of strategic planning when certain elements were present. A vast number of strategic plans were analyzed and rated on specific dimensions of planning, implementing, and monitoring. In summary of their findings, plans that were rated higher on the dimensions measured showed higher gains in student achievement. One of the most remarkable findings was the outcome regarding expectations. In the schools where educators held high expectations for student achievement and attributed success to their work with the students, performance was significantly better than in schools where educators attributed achievement to student demographic data, such as socioeconomic status, gender, or race.

In addition to expectations, the monitoring and evaluation dimensions were important. Schools whose plans scored high in frequency of monitoring, meaning progress was monitored at least monthly, analyzed a variety of data sources, including student performance, teaching strategies, and leadership practices. The data used for analysis were current and timely. These schools did not wait for year-end assessment data and hope that their strategies increased achievement. Rather, data were reviewed often so that adjustments could be made along the way. High scores on the evaluation dimension meant that schools continuously asked the question, is it working? When the answer was no, schools discontinued or modified those practices or strategies. Educators at schools with high marks in the area of evaluation had a clear understanding of how their professional practice impacted student achievement and they utilized strategies that were shown to be successful in improving outcomes.

The findings support two theories that were postulated nearly fifty years ago that are relevant in education today, namely, the Pygmalion effect and the attribution theory. The Pygmalion effect maintains that expectations about a person can lead to the person behaving in a manner as to confirm those expectations. As an example, a teacher can be told that he has been assigned a class of gifted students to start the new school year, even though the class is actually a heterogeneously grouped class. The teacher will treat the students differently, perhaps by providing more attention and support and by expecting them to achieve at higher levels. Generally, students live up to those expectations.

The attribution theory maintains that a person attributes success or failure to certain factors. The theoretical framework of the attribution theory, developed by Bernard Weiner, speaks to three areas: locus, stability, and controllability. Locus deals with the location of the cause, either internal or external to the person. Stability relates to whether the cause is likely to stay the same or change in the near future. Controllability concerns whether or not the person can control the cause. To illustrate the theory, consider a student who is failing in a class. If the student operates with an external locus of control, he will attribute the failure to an outside cause, such as the teacher. On the other hand, for a student operating with an internal locus of control, he will understand that his lack of effort could be the reason for poor performance.

In the second area, stability, a student failing a math class would hold the belief that he has never been good at math; therefore, he is failing the math class now. If the student believes that conceivably the environment could change, the student would believe that he may be able to pass the math class next time with appropriate effort and assistance. The third area, controllability, is more of an emotional response. If a student feels responsible for his failure, he may feel guilty, or if he feels responsible for his success, he may feel proud. Controllability deals with whether or not the student can control the cause. For example, if a basketball player is an excellent free-throw shooter, he may feel proud because he has put a great deal of time and effort into practicing, which is something he can control.

Both the Pygmalion effect and the attribution theory are relevant to school improvement and to the strategic planning process. In addition to developing a great strategic plan, you must also develop the approaches staff members will use in building relationships with students. This will ensure their attitudes toward students and beliefs about students are aligned with the mission and vision of the school. At some point during the planning process, you should devote time to this effort whether as a professional development topic with your staff or individually with specific staff members. Staff members should become familiar with the two theories presented here and possibly others you believe to be relevant to your particular situation. The importance of these theories cannot be overstated. Teachers who believe that students can excel even if, for example, they come from low socioeconomic backgrounds play an essential role in the success of the improvement plan. Your staff must possess the proper mind-set to approach this process. Principals can have the greatest, most innovative plan, but unless they have an effective staff, the plan will not survive. Outstanding principals know that it is the people, not the programs, who make the difference. With this in mind, be sure to do everything possible to assist struggling teachers improve their instruction in order to meet the needs of their students. Incorporating a variety of professional development opportunities can boost performance as well as the morale of your staff.

Planning Timeframe

Creating a timeline for the planning process will assist in keeping it firmly on track. When you set out to create a strategic plan, you can count on spending from a few months to a year in the planning phase prior to beginning the implementation of the plan. The planning phase encompasses the following:

- defining the purpose
- selecting and organizing the school planning team
- gathering input from the staff, parents, and community
- creating the mission and vision statements
- setting the goals
- gathering and analyzing data
- writing the plan
- communicating the plan with the school community

During the course of the planning phase, collaboration and participation are essential. People will feel they are part of and will be supportive of the process when there is involvement from the beginning. This is especially true in the planning phase because what goes into the plan will affect the staff's daily work.

A planning timeline is presented in chapter 2. The timeframe for the implementation of the strategic planning process can vary, but most strategic plans are created for a three-year cycle. A longer or shorter period ranging from one to ten years may be appropriate in the business sector; however, three years is an optimal length of time to implement a strategic plan in the school setting. The process should be long enough to ensure the strategies are implemented according to plan and that the strategies initiated have had a sufficient amount of time to demonstrate their merit. The timeframe should not be too lengthy because, as discussed earlier, the ever changing environment in education may require new strategies. Maintaining current strategies that are not working would be unproductive. Keep in mind that although a plan may be prepared for three years, periodic updates will be in place to review progress. Revisions can be made at the point of the reviews as appropriate. A three-year plan truly allows the school to skillfully implement new strategies and practices. As you develop the plan, keep in mind that all strategies will most likely not be implemented during the first year. There are instances when the first year is all about researching a specific program or strategy and then the second year begins the implementation phase. It is important to be aware of this because the tendency will be to start every new initiative the first year. This can lead to the demise of the plan because too much change at once can be overwhelming. All strategies cannot be implemented at one time if the process is to succeed. Therefore, the timeline is a major consideration.

As you approach the middle of the third year of implementation, you should begin to consider what will happen at the end of your current three-year plan. Discussions should take place regarding the next three-year plan. This is the time to convene a new school planning team (SPT), be it the original members, a new team altogether, or a combination of both. While all of the three-year data will not be available for evaluation, the team should have solid evidence from the first two years and the quarterly reviews from the third year as a basis for developing the strategies for the new plan that will go into effect at the beginning of the fourth year (the first year of the second plan). You can imagine that subsequent plans will be much easier to create once you have been through the process. Nonetheless, all phases of the process need to be revisited including a review of the mission and vision. Goals, strategies, and action steps may be continued, modified, or newly created depending upon the results you have achieved based on the evidence from your analysis of the data.

Elements of the Strategic Plan

Elements of a strategic planning process are linear as well as cyclical and interdependent upon one another. The steps are considered to be linear because they need to be followed in sequence to make sure that the plan is approached in an organized manner, is complete, and covers all areas comprehensively. Each step involves utilizing organizational resources, such as money, programs, or human inputs that transform the information into useful outputs. The outputs will function as the input for the next stage of the process. Information is gathered from the staff and school community to create the purpose, mission, vision, and goals. With completing the first step, the output becomes the purpose, mission statement, vision statement, and goals. These are used as the basis for the second step, data collection and analysis. Utilizing the results of the data collection and analysis, the third step, writing the plan, takes place and the output is the written strategic plan. The written plan is the input for the fourth step, implementing the plan. The output is the actual use of strategies and action plans. The fifth step, monitoring and evaluating progress, produces results as the output. Finally, using the results achieved, the sixth step, revising the plan, is conducted based on the results achieved. The output from this step is the revised plan which then becomes the input as you return to step four, implementing the plan. Figure 1.2 illustrates the planning steps.

Strategic Planning Flowchart

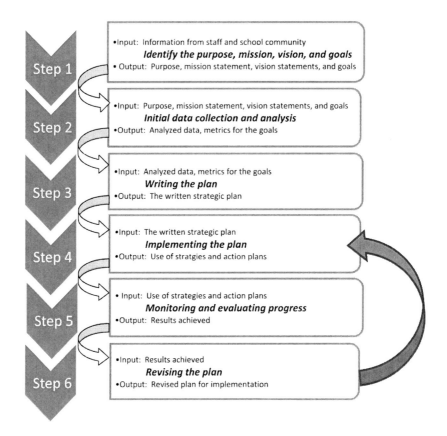

Figure 1.2. The strategic planning model displayed in a linear format.

The cyclical characteristic of the process occurs as you move throughout the various stages. As monitoring and evaluation activities are being performed at predetermined points during the implementation of the plan, such as monthly or quarterly, some aspects of the plan may need to be revised. It is necessary to go back through the stages of the process as this review takes place to determine what ought to be changed and to be certain the new changes align with the mission, vision, and goals. It is important to stick to the original strategies that were researched and developed for the plan, if at all possible, because these initiatives were aligned with the mission, vision, and goals in the beginning and changes can sometimes stray from the original intent. Unless you determine a strategy is completely unsuitable, you need to allow sufficient time for the strategy to demonstrate its value. The revising stage should not be viewed as a time to start over; nonetheless, the strategies should be discussed, evaluated, and possibly be modified. As revisions of the plan take shape, the plan will be amended and you will move from step six, revising the plan, around to step four, implementing the plan, as shown in figure 1.3. Once the plan is initially implemented, it is not necessary to start over from the beginning after revisions are made to the plan during the three-year cycle. You will move from the sixth step (revising the plan) to the fourth step (implementing the plan) to the fifth step (monitoring and evaluating the plan) and once again to the sixth step (revising the plan). It is not necessary to go back through steps one and two because your purpose, mission, vision, and goals will not change during the implementation of the three-year plan; however, you will reference these steps as you make revisions. The data collection and analysis will be handled through the monitoring and evaluating phase.

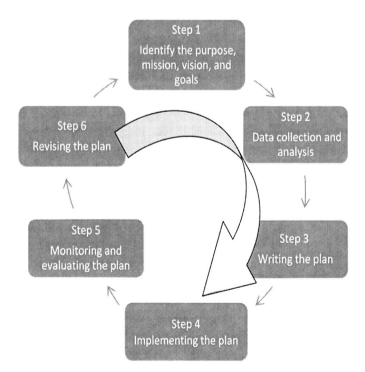

Figure 1.3 The strategic planning model displayed in a cyclical format.

The Value of Strategic Planning

You have taken the first step toward true leadership by embracing strategic planning. You, as the instructional leader, need to rally your entire staff around this process and together believe that what you do will truly impact student learning in your building. The value of strategic planning cannot be overstated, particularly in these times of accountability. Good planning can be the difference between maintaining the status quo and realizing high achievement. To make the most of your plan, a razor-sharp focus must be placed on the strategies within the plan while ensuring consistent implementation. This is an area that illustrates the point regarding all facets of the organization being involved not only in the implementation of the plan but also in the creation of the plan. Everyone must accept his role in terms of implementation of the plan to maximize success.

A strategic plan can be a powerful tool for school improvement on many fronts. Academic as well as social aspects of your building can be addressed that can produce huge dividends for years to come. As strategies are implemented, they become a new way of doing business because what is included in the plan will replace old approaches with newly created strategies. You are not adding to the workload but streamlining the work with more effective tools. It is imperative that members of the school community understand this concept prior to the start of the planning process since most people commonly perceive that something new means doing something more. The goal for everyone is, as the saying goes, to work smarter, not harder. Strategic planning can be the mechanism for accomplishing this goal.

Strategic planning can provide significant value to your school in a number of ways. Most importantly, strategic planning can serve as a method of clearly defining the purpose and goals of the organization. In addition, it can provide the direction needed for meeting the goals. Compare the planning process to planning a trip using a global positioning system (GPS) device. Especially when traveling in unchartered territory, you need to have specific directions (strategies) and explicit steps (action plans) to arrive at the proper destination (goals). You must know where you are going if you want to get there. Your GPS will guide you as you make your way to your destination (implementing the plan). The device also gives you additional information to assist along the way. For example, the GPS will tell you how much time the trip will take and the number of miles to get there (monitoring). The GPS can guide you through construction and detours (revising). Likewise, with your strategic plan, a clear direction with a specified purpose and precise goals can help even the most difficult school improve.

Utilizing a strategic plan eliminates the variability of what teachers are using in their classrooms. At times, teachers may hear of new programs or ideas they want to try with their students. While no principal wants to discourage creativity, innovation, or a teacher's enthusiasm, a strategic planning process will assist your school in handling this type of situation. If a certain strategy has been decided upon through your planning process, for example, a specific writing process at a selected grade level, all teachers need to follow the specified process. You do not want a teacher going out on his own trying another method during the implementation phase. When the planning team takes the time to identify and select a program, process, or procedure, it needs to be implemented by everyone according to the plans in order to determine its effectiveness later on. This speaks to the need to involve all staff in the planning process and to bring innovative ideas to the table. The ideas should be discussed among the planning team and with the teachers who will implement them in order to select the most appropriate strategies. This will also help to gain widespread ownership of the strategies that have been selected for implementation.

To illustrate this point, think about a math department of eight members discussing a strategy they will use. Will a first-year teacher react to the strategy the same as a ten-year or twenty-year veteran? For instance, a new teacher may be excited to implement the strategy whereas the veteran teacher may not be as receptive. The veteran teacher might want to hold on to a strategy she has used in the past, or she may respond, "We've tried that before and it didn't work." As stated previously, all ideas should be given consideration. Perhaps the reasons the ideas didn't work in the past were because everyone did not implement them correctly or because some teachers may not have implemented them at all. If the veteran teacher can support her strategy with results, it may be a viable option to consider. There should be consensus among the teachers based on evidence of the effectiveness of the strategy. You want all eight teachers in the department implementing what has been decided upon. Innovative ideas can and should be incorporated into the plan, and teachers should be encouraged to share their ideas for consideration, especially if they have been using a strategy that has shown to be effective. Ideas that are not used at this time can be recorded for use at another time.

Opportunities for teachers to be a part of the process will result in greater acceptance and implementation of the plan. The practice of involving the teachers will generate enthusiasm for the plan due to the fact that they are a part of the process. A strategic plan does not mean instruction will be dull and boring. On the contrary, it can be the catalyst for bringing energy and excitement to your school in a practical, methodical fashion.

Strategic planning mitigates crisis management. When you use this approach in your building, you will have an organized and systematic manner in which to accomplish your goals. With strategic planning, you will not only create but also implement processes for dealing with routine issues. To illustrate this point, think back to the introduction to this book. Did you see yourself in the description? Are you finding yourself running—literally—from one crisis or disruption to another? To deal with these issues, one of your goals may deal with the climate of your building. To improve the climate, you need to have routines and procedures in place for handling various situations. By maintaining focus throughout the duration of the plan, the school will benefit from greater efficiency and effectiveness. Thus, you will not fall into the trap of "putting out fires." In other words, you will not need to be continually responding to crises or urgent matters.

The planning process generally will lead to stronger teamwork, cohesiveness, and unity among members of the staff. By planning together, staff will form stronger working relationships, build closer bonds with other department or team members, and develop an appreciation for the work of others. Regardless of their position, staff members will become more comfortable talking about ideas and strategies with one another. The process can generate a sense of ownership, which in turn can translate into trust and respect.

Representation on the SPT from all areas of the building helps to ensure complete buy-in; therefore, staff members from within various teams and departments need to be included on the planning team. Once planning is complete, all teachers and staff members need to shoulder the responsibility of implementing the strategic plan.

Utilizing a broad range of human resources in the planning process will result in a comprehensive plan. The perspective of different points of view must be represented so that a complete picture can be appreciated. The perspective of a math teacher will be much different than the perspective of a secretary, for example, yet each will provide valuable input that otherwise may not be considered. You can see the sense of pride when a custodian, secretary, or paraprofessional is asked to be a part of the process. They will be amazed, first of all, that they were invited, and second, what is even more important is the fact that they can make a difference in many crucial ways that the educators may not be able to. These individuals many times know about issues before the principal or teachers. Let's consider for a moment the building secretary. The secretary is most often the first person to greet a parent or community member who comes into the building or to take care of a student who comes to the office. Through participating as a member of the team, the secretary will be more likely to take greater pride in the work and can be an ambassador to parents and community members. Consider the custodian as a member of the planning team. The custodian is largely responsible for the safety of students and staff by making certain the building is in good repair and by making certain that cleaning and maintenance issues are handled in a timely manner. Taking part on the planning team will give the custodian the sense that his work is extremely important to the overall success of the school. Furthermore, there are distinctive types of people—some are thinkers and some are doers. Combine them with a variety of personality types who bring their own knowledge, background, experiences, and attitudes to the table and the team will not lack for lively discussion.

The community will also benefit from the collegial relationships and communication that are developed with the school staff. The community will be aware of what is going on in the school, and partnerships can develop that will benefit both the community and the school. Community resources should be built into the plan.

Strategic planning makes good sense from a business perspective. Financial resources can be directed to specific areas based on the needs stated in the strategic plan. Resources will then be used for the school's stated priorities and therefore can be allocated to fund the initiatives stated in the plan. As the plan is monitored, you can determine whether or not the financial resources are utilized in the best possible manner.

Finally, strategic planning can serve as a means of determining progress. For accountability purposes, a strategic plan will serve to demonstrate not only academic results but also the success of certain strategies. Performance measures should be identified, and the measures should be tied to the goals in order to place the focus on results. The strategies need to be consistently monitored and then evaluated so that educators can decide whether or not a strategy brought about the desired results and whether a strategy should be continued, modified, or terminated. The process will serve as a basis for measurement to help formulate future strategic planning.

The Value of Strategic Planning

> ➤ Defined purpose and goals
> ➤ Direction for the school
> ➤ Fidelity of instruction
> ➤ Mitigation of crisis management
> ➤ Clarification of roles and responsibilities
> ➤ Teacher involvement, collaboration, and teamwork
> ➤ Improved community relations
> ➤ Better utilization of financial resources
> ➤ Determination of progress
> ➤ Accountability

Time Management

Often you will hear people say they are too busy or don't have time for something new. While you know it is the right thing to do, it may be a challenge to convince your staff that the strategic planning efforts will actually prove to be beneficial to them in the long run. It is critical that you change the culture of the school and the mind-set of the staff by focusing on the results that are achieved, not on how hard people work. Everyone is held accountable for results, not just efforts. Meetings or professional development sessions devoted to the discussion of time management would be valuable to conduct with the staff to move them toward thinking strategically and, again, working smarter not harder. There are numerous resources on time management. To illustrate one, here is an effective exercise to conduct with the staff that will help them realize the types of activities that can essentially be viewed as time wasters. Staff members can learn to use their time more appropriately. Use the following eight-item survey and the activity that accompanies the survey to emphasize the importance of good time management. Here is how to conduct the activity.

> ➤ Provide every staff member with a copy of the eight-item survey. Ask the staff to complete the survey individually using the scale 1-6 as shown below the survey items.

1. I spend much of my time on important activities that demand my immediate attention, such as pressing problems and deadline-driven projects.
2. I feel I am always "putting out fires" and working in crisis mode.
3. I feel I waste a lot of time.
4. I spend much of my time on activities that have little relevance to my top priorities but demand my immediate attention (interruptions, unimportant meetings, phone calls, e-mails).
5. I spend much of my time on activities that are important, such as planning, preparation, prevention, relationship building, and self-renewal.
6. I spend much of my time on busywork, compulsive habits, junk mail, excessive TV, Internet, games, etc.
7. I feel I am on top of things because of careful preparation, planning, and prevention.
8. I feel I am constantly addressing issues that are important to others but not to me.

1. Strongly Disagree, 2. Disagree, 3. Slightly Disagree, 4. Slightly Agree, 5. Agree, 6. Strongly Agree

> ➤ Once the survey is completed, each person will add his or her scores from each of the items in the following manner:
> (*I* stands for *item*)

I1 + I2 = _____
I4 + I8 = _____
I5 + I7 = _____
I3 + I6 = _____

> ➤ After the scores are totaled, show this four quadrant Time Management Matrix diagram. Have each person place his or her score in the quadrants as shown.

Time Management Matrix

I	II
I1 + I2 =	I5 + I7 =
III	**IV**
I4 + I8 =	I3 + I6 =

> ➤ Once the scores are placed in the corresponding quadrants, ask staff members to identify their quadrant with the highest score. Present the following chart. Have the staff members find the information in the quadrant each has scored the highest. Share the descriptors and corresponding information (below) about each of the quadrants.

Time Management Matrix

	Urgent	Not Urgent
Important	**I** • Crises • Pressing problem • Deadline driven-projects, meetings • Reactive tasks **The quadrant of "daily reality"**	**II** • Preparations • Presentations • Relationship building • True recreation • Proactive tasks **The quadrant of "quality"**
Not Important	**III** • Interruptions • Some phone calls, mail, reports • Many proximate pressing matters • Many popular activities **The quadrant of "deception"**	**IV** • Trivia • Junk mail • Some phone calls • Time wasters • "Escape" activities • Mindless activities **The quadrant of "waste"**

(*Source:* Covey, 1994, *First Things First*)

Quadrant I (Urgent, Important)

People need to spend time in this quadrant; however, operating too often or too long in this quadrant can cause a great deal of stress in your life. Activities associated with this quadrant are responding to emergencies, crisis management, crisis resolution, deadline-driven projects, and pressing problems. Generally, the results you will see from working in this quadrant are crisis management, always putting out fires, stress, and burn-out.

Quadrant II (Not Urgent, Important)

When people function in this quadrant, they utilize excellent management skills and have found a way to balance responsibilities.

Activities associated with this quadrant include planning, prevention, and building relationships. Generally, the results you will see from working in this quadrant are vision, discipline, control, and few crises. You will reap the most rewards in the long run by operating more of the time in this quadrant.

Quadrant III (Urgent, Not Important)

When people function in this quadrant, they find themselves spinning their wheels. They seem to be busy but never seem to accomplish the important tasks. Activities associated with this quadrant are interruptions, some phone calls, some e-mails, pressing matters, and minor tasks. Generally, the results you will see from working in this quadrant are crisis management, shallow relationships, feeling of being out of control, and seeing goals and plans as worthless. You want to minimize the amount of time spent in this quadrant.

Quadrant IV (Not Urgent, Not Important)

When people function in this quadrant, they are escaping from the reality of their work. Activities associated with this quadrant are busywork, some phone calls, some e-mails, and using social media. Generally, the results you will see from working in this quadrant are dependency on others, irresponsibility, and loss of employment. You should greatly minimize or eliminate the time spent in this quadrant.

Summary of the Time Management Activity

From these quadrant descriptions, it is clear to see that staff should attempt to function primarily in Quadrant II, realizing that there are still occasions that Quadrants I, III, and IV will be utilized. As professionals who are striving to improve student academic achievement, time spent in Quadrant II will better assist them in reaching the efficiency and effectiveness that is essential to achieving the goals. Staff should focus on Quadrant II for long-term achievement of goals and to minimize the amount of time they spend in Quadrants I, III, and IV.

Participants in this activity will gain a better understanding of their personal style in dealing with day-to-day tasks and responsibilities. Knowing and doing what is important rather than simply responding to what is urgent is crucial if staff members wish to improve their time management skills and, therefore, results. You will find that most teachers and staff members have not given much thought to how they manage their time. Most would probably argue that they need to respond to the needs that arise during the day with their students. While this is true, there are ways to change the culture of classrooms and schools by placing the focus on that which is most important, thereby minimizing the time spent on time wasters and reactive tasks.

By setting the groundwork with activities such as this, you will start to open the door for change. While this is a very brief introduction to time management, staff members will begin to recognize the value of thinking and working strategically to increase their capacity to effect change. You and your staff should pursue additional information on this topic as necessary.

Chapter Summary

The notion of strategic planning as a school improvement process is one that ought to be considered by schools and districts everywhere. While preparing the strategic plan is a critical piece of the process, what you do prior to planning is equally important. You must lay the groundwork with your staff so that everyone on your team will be prepared for the changes ahead. Educational research can provide the foundation on which to build support. By presenting topics for discussion such as the Pygmalion effect and the attribution theory as offered in this chapter, you can develop a climate that is conducive to change.

Strategic planning can be the vehicle for bringing about improvements in your school. Among some of the benefits, strategic planning can define your purpose and goals, provide direction for your school, clarify roles and responsibilities, improve collaboration and teamwork, and foster accountability.

Involving your staff in strategic planning entails changing the culture and accepting responsibility for results. The best research-based strategies or the most creative ideas may prove to be unsuccessful if the right conditions are not in place. To ensure success, allow a sufficient amount of time to prepare the staff for the process and to build a quality strategic plan.

Addressing the topic of time management with your staff can lead to greater usage of strategic thinking and can open the door to changing the culture of the school. Efficiency and effectiveness can be improved as professionals operate in Quadrant II of the Time Management Matrix.

CHAPTER 2

Planning Steps

Whether looking to make improvements in the daily operations of your school building or improvements in student achievement, approaching an improvement course of action from a strategic planning standpoint is vital to your success. Regardless of the issue at hand, results will be greatly enhanced when a strategic plan is implemented. The planning process, when completed thoroughly, can take from several months to as long as a year to accomplish. It is not something to take lightly or to hurry through. When principals decide strategic planning is appropriate, they many times face the urgency of demonstrating growth in student achievement, which may seem to dictate a quicker pace. Rushing through the steps of the plan or jumping directly to the strategies phase can undermine the process. Shortcuts will jeopardize the plan down the road so do not be tempted to circumvent the process.

Since the time that strategic planning was adapted from business models for education, little has been done to create a standard model for educators to follow. Neither has strategic planning been recommended as a school improvement model. While there still are limited resources on strategic planning approaches specifically for educators, most of the information consists of similar key steps designed to help an organization reach its identified goals and objectives. Although strategic planning approaches for education follow a pattern similar to those used in business settings, outcomes differ for each setting. In business, outcomes center on sales and profits. Educational outcomes center on measures in student learning and achievement levels and, therefore, the achievement of the school. The process is especially difficult when dealing with the outcomes in education as compared to business measures because there are a greater number of factors in the educational setting that impact outcomes, such as the learning differences and ability levels of individual students. For example, eighth-grade students in one school taking a state achievement test may enter the testing situation with a wide range of achievement levels. Furthermore, eighth-grade students throughout a given state come from a variety of settings, such as urban or rural, and have varied experiences, which influence their success on a statewide assessment. There are differences in the students' past academic achievement, grades, attendance, motivation, and the like, (inputs) that will impact the results (outputs or outcomes) of the assessments.

The process of creating the strategic plan is as important as the plan itself. In order to get the most out of your school or district's strategic planning process, the plan must be approached with a high level of trust among the administration, staff, and school community. Common ground must be reached during the first phase of the process when you identify and define the purpose, mission, vision, and goals. After successfully reaching consensus in these areas, the next phase of the planning process can begin. If you see that frequent difficulties arise in the process of gaining consensus, it may be best to take a step back and work on staff relations, trust, and collaboration before going any further. Although you will be adding to the amount of time needed to create the plan, it will be time well spent as the process will progress much more smoothly when good communication and collaboration are present. If you are concerned about staff relations and communication even prior to beginning your strategic planning process, take the time beforehand to deal with such issues. By taking the time in advance, the process will operate more effectively and with fewer problems in the long run. You can find a number of resources available on this topic to assist you.

Throughout the development of the strategic plan, new ideas may emerge that need to be considered. The planning team must establish whether or not the new ideas should be addressed immediately or whether they should be held for consideration at a later time. A "parking lot" can be a tool to help you organize new ideas. The ideas are recorded on chart paper that is posted on the wall during each meeting. As thoughts and ideas emerge, you will find that some do not fit with the current discussion but are important to capture for use at a later time. Record these ideas on the parking lot chart. While there may be other ways to record ideas, the parking lot chart is recommended for use as a visual reminder during meetings. This may appear to be a small point, however, even the most innocuous matter could derail a meeting and valuable time could be lost. Be sure to establish this process in the early stages and use it regularly during the planning meetings.

The Model

The steps in the strategic planning model are: identifying the purpose, mission, vision, and goals; collecting and analyzing data; writing the plan; implementing the plan; monitoring and evaluating progress; and revising the plan. If you are already involved in a school improvement process, as most schools are, you can still benefit greatly from following this model. If a process or plan is already in place for your building, you can incorporate the two documents together. This way, you can meet the requirements for your district or state, for example, and you can also address the needs of the building that you have determined are important.

The strategic plan described here is a more thorough and detailed document than a school-improvement plan used by most schools because of the inclusion of action plans. Most improvement plans do not include the detailed step of writing action plans but only include goals and the strategies to accomplish the goals. As you will see in later chapters, with this strategic planning model, you will be able to make the desired improvements much more quickly due to the addition of the action plans. The model for organizing and the method of developing the action plan component will be introduced in chapter 5.

This planning model was created specifically for principals and leadership teams who aspire to affect change. It can easily be adapted to a segment of a school district, such as all elementary schools within a district, or an entire school district by making modifications to the planning team which are discussed later in this chapter. The process herein has been created for use in educational environments and is recommended as a strategy to implement for school improvement. Each step will be examined in subsequent chapters. The following illustration provides a visual overview of the planning model indicating that the purpose, mission, and vision funnel together to form the basis for creating the goals. From there, the process continues through the remaining steps.

Strategic Planning Process Model

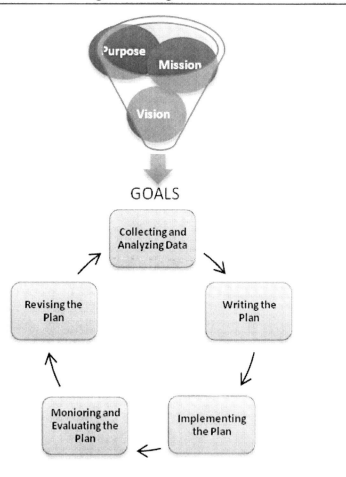

Figure 2.1. Strategic planning model.

Timeline

Approach the strategic planning process with a firm timeline. The building principal, and perhaps other members of the administration or staff, should create a timeline to be followed by the planning team. Without a set timeframe in which to prepare the plan, interest can wane. If people perceive the planning process as too long or cumbersome, they will surely be less inclined to commit to the process. In addition, consider the most appropriate time during the school year to begin the planning process. If, for instance, you wish to implement the plan at the beginning of a new school year, start the planning process as early as September but no later than January of the current school year. Be sure to budget time for members of the team to both seek input on upcoming topics and to report back to their departments or teams. A sufficient amount of time will allow you to be certain that a solid plan is developed that will be ready for implementation, such as that illustrated on the following timeline.

Planning Timeline

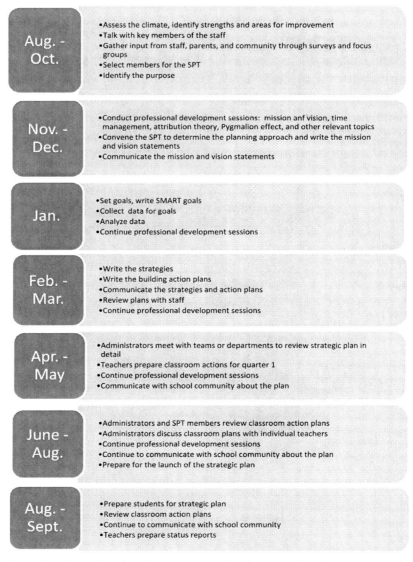

Figure 2.2. Planning timeline: preparing for the strategic planning process.

Preparing for the Planning Process

In preparation for undertaking this strategic planning process, a discussion on change is imperative. Prior to beginning your planning, thoughtful consideration must be given to how the change will be approached and managed. Using the "strategic planning" terminology will cause some people to get excited about the prospect, some to become wary, and others to resist right from the start. There will be an assortment of reactions when news of the impending process is released, so you want to set the stage prior to discussing the plan. Talk with key people on the staff. Use those who are excited about the process to help spread a positive message to others. Work with those you know will be resistant to this change to help them feel at ease. Understand that if you create the strategic plan solely as an administrative function, the process will most likely fail. If you force change on your staff, problems are bound to occur. You want the staff to be prepared for and embrace the change as well as participate in the process. Here are some keys to doing just that:

- Remember that most people fear and are resistant to change.
- Be proactive, start conversations about the process early.
- Be open, keep lines of communication open.
- Identify the needs of the school as seen through the eyes of the staff.
- Consult with leaders among the staff about the process.
- Be inclusive of all staff and school community.
- Do not impose the change on the staff.

The Planning Team

Once you have laid the groundwork, you are ready to formulate your planning team. Since the focus in this book is on individual school plans, you can refer to your team as the school planning team (SPT). Developing the SPT requires great consideration. The team should consist of approximately twelve to twenty people comprised of key members of the school community, including administrators, teachers, parents, students (if appropriate), and community representatives. The inclusion of student members on the planning team should be strongly considered. Student members ought to be considered at the high school level and perhaps at the middle school level. Elementary students may not be able to handle the meeting situations and schedule of the team but should at the least be given consideration or be included in other ways. A quality strategic plan cannot and should not be created without essential members of the organization participating in the process. Key people among the staff must be involved, however, not to the exclusion of others. While every staff member cannot be involved in every phase of the process, it is important to be inclusive, meaning staff from among various departments or grade levels, for example, should be included. You will find that staff members value an inclusive approach because they will be a part of the process and they will know that their input is important. When their ideas and concerns are expressed in constructive ways, the process will be meaningful for all involved. Once people have a voice and feel that their input matters, there will be greater buy-in and much better implementation of the strategies, and hence, better results. The fundamental point is to be inclusive without going to the extreme. If too many people are involved in the SPT, the process can become overwhelming and trying. To ensure an appropriate balance, seek representation from across all areas of the school community. In a high school setting, for example, you need teachers, support staff, community members, and possibly, students to be a part of the SPT along with the principal. An additional administrator is advisable if the building is large, otherwise, you as the instructional leader will be the administrator on the SPT. This is an important responsibility as the building leader and is not a responsibility you want to delegate.

While the information presented in this book focuses primarily on the individual school building plan, this strategic planning process can assist an entire district in creating a comprehensive plan as well. For a districtwide plan, a district planning team (DPT) should be created and members of the team should come together for planning meetings. At the opening meeting, the superintendent along with other district leaders should present the timeline and a schedule for subsequent meetings to be held throughout the planning process. The DPT members should, as part of the team, make the commitment to attend and participate in all meetings. The priority for the process must be emphasized in order to complete the plan in a timely manner. Between scheduled meetings, representatives serving on the team will report back to their specific buildings, departments, or divisions and seek input on future topics.

The size of the district will dictate the number of members and perhaps the configuration of the planning team. Large districts may need to subdivide by levels or by geographic areas, such as feeder patterns. The large district group will proceed in the same manner as that of a small district with one main difference. The difference is that a group comprised of liaisons from each of the subgroups along with the superintendent and other district administrators will meet. Then, with information from this meeting, the liaisons will be responsible for conducting meetings with their respective subgroups. The liaisons are charged with the task of maintaining communication with the district group as well as their individual subgroup. The liaison will be responsible for taking the ideas generated in the subgroup meetings to the district team and will be the point person for reporting from the district group back to the individual subgroup. The subgroup members will then work with their respective buildings to craft their own strategic plan based on the district goals.

A medium or small district should include representatives from all buildings and include community members, parents, and students, if appropriate. The members selected would comprise the planning team and participate in all aspects of the process. No matter the size or configuration of the planning team, the important point is to maintain an open dialogue and continue to maintain inclusiveness in the process. District level planning teams should generally range in size from fifteen members to twenty-five members. If more members are needed in order to be inclusive, the district should consider subdividing into smaller groups and then follow the pattern of the large district planning team.

District Planning Teams

The following figures illustrate possible configurations of district strategic planning teams in small, medium, or large districts. In the first example, the small school district is comprised of one high school, one middle school, and four elementary schools. The superintendent and at least one other central office administrator should be included on the team. The remainder of the team should be comprised of the building principal from each building, a teacher or staff representative from each building, one or two parent or community representatives from each building, and student representatives. The configuration of the DPT for a small district should look something like this.

Small School District

Superintendent
Central office administrator
High school principal
Middle school principal
Elementary school principals
Teacher or staff representatives
(one from each school)
Parent and community representatives
(one to two from each school)
Student representatives

Figure 2.3. Small school district planning team.

In the second example, the medium school district is comprised of three high schools, five middle schools, and ten elementary schools. The superintendent and at least two other central office administrators should be included on the team. The remainder of the team should be comprised of the principal from each building, a teacher or staff representative from each building, and a parent or community member from each building. Since this is a very large group, you could consider dividing the group into two subgroups in the same fashion as the large district described below. The configuration of the DPT for a medium school district should look something like this.

Medium School District

Superintendent
Central Office Administrators (two)
Building Principals
(one from each school, total of eighteen)
A teacher or staff representative from each building
A parent or community member from each building
Student representatives

Figure 2.4. Medium school district planning team.

In the third example, the large school district is comprised of twelve high schools, twenty middle schools, and forty elementary schools. The superintendent and, if the district is set up in divisions or areas, the lead administrator for each area should be included on the team. To maintain a reasonable size for the team, subgroups should be formed, and liaisons from each subgroup will serve on the main district planning team. The configuration of the DPT for a large school district should look something like this.

Large School District

District Planning Team
Superintendent
Central office administrator from each subgroup
One principal liaisons from each subgroup
One teacher or staff representative from each group
Two parent or community member liaisons from each subgroup
Student liaisons from each group

Subgroup 1	Subgroup 2	Subgroup 3	Subgroup 4
Central office adm.	Central office adm.	Central office adm.	Central office adm.
Three HS principals	Three HS principals	Three HS principals	Three HS principals
Five MS principals	Five MS principals	Five MS principals	Five MS principals
Ten Elem. Principals	Ten Elem. Principals	Ten Elem. Principals	Ten Elem. Principals
Teacher or staff rep.	Teacher or staff rep.	Teacher or staff rep.	Teacher or staff rep.
Parent and community rep.	Parent and community rep.	Parent and community rep.	Parent and community rep.
Student rep.	Student rep.	Student rep.	Student rep.

Figure 2.5. District planning team for a large district.

Selecting the School Planning Team

There are a number of ways to go about selecting a planning team. The members you choose should be forward thinking, meaning they need to be able to help set a course for the future. The members should also be strategic thinking individuals who understand the relationship between quality planning and achieving results. Think about the method you would prefer to use to build your planning team. You could

    a. enlist current leadership, which could consist of department chairs or team leaders, for example;
    b. ask for volunteers from the staff and building community;
    c. hand-pick or appoint members you want on the team; and
    d. use a combination of all three.

Which one did you choose? Let's look at each one individually to examine the viability of such a planning team.

Enlist Current Leadership

Selecting choice "a" would be a more traditional approach and perhaps, a choice that many would select. You could reason that these staff members are already leaders in the school with experience and presumably the respect of their peers. While this may seem to be a valid choice, consider what might be missing. Current leadership could mean different things. It could be the informal leadership or those perceived as having the power and influence. It could be those on a current advisory committee. Your building may have an elected group of leaders serving on a leadership team. The leadership could even be those appointed to positions, such as department heads or team leaders. Previously, I discussed this process as inclusive. If only the current leaders are used, you may be leaving out someone who is interested or highly motivated to serve on this team. The current leaders may not be interested in taking on this responsibility because they may already have a full plate and not have the time to devote to this endeavor. In addition, all areas of the building community may not be represented with this approach.

Ask for Volunteers

Selecting choice "b" would ensure that the members of the team really want to be there. This could also be a good choice, but again there are drawbacks to this method. Think about the individual who is hardworking, creative, full of great ideas, and wonderful at working with students. This may be a teacher who is very comfortable around students but somewhat fearful of working on an important team such as this. This type of individual could be an asset to the team but may need to be coaxed to participate. There may be individuals with particular expertise that you want to have on the team who may not volunteer. Again, with this method, you may not have all areas of the building community represented.

Appoint Members

Selecting choice "c" may work best for you as the leader. However, don't be tempted to go this route. Even though you know your staff and would most likely have the greatest knowledge of who would work well on the team, this could prove to be the approach least likely to succeed. While you could ensure an inclusive team by selecting members from all areas of the school community, this approach brings out other problems. The staff could perceive this as playing favorites or some may wonder why they were not selected and other individuals were. As you know, as an administrator, you are never going to be able to please everyone. But if you do select this approach, be prepared to respond to concerns by letting people know you appreciate their interest and let them know there are other ways in which they may assist during the process.

Use a Combination

Selecting choice "d" is the advisable method to use when building your strategic planning team. Of all the choices listed, you are able to build the best team you possibly can by means of a combination of the three. You need some members to have leadership experience. Therefore, you should have four to five current leaders on the team. You need to have individuals who are enthusiastic and who want to be involved, so you certainly want a portion of the team to be made up of volunteers. Seek volunteers from the staff and make a list of those who offer to serve on the team. You should then be the one to select a set number of people from the list of volunteers. But most importantly, you are held accountable for your school's results. Therefore, the members you appoint should be chosen wisely. You want staff members who are creative, intelligent, visionary, dependable, approachable, and communicative in this group you will appoint. The appointed members need to blend with the leadership segment and the volunteer segment to ensure that a quality plan is developed.

In any case, you need to retain the final say in who serves on the team. Your team must include members who will be respected by the staff, be able to support your overall vision for the plan, and complete the work in a timely manner.

Approaches to Strategic Planning

Strategic planning is not a one-size-fits-all endeavor. Although there are particular stages or phases within the planning process that are indeed similar across various approaches, the plan should be built based on needs of your particular building. While there should be a high level of individualization, similarities do exist in the stages of the process that are necessary and should be conducted following a common sequence. The uniqueness will be apparent in your own goals, strategies, and action plans developed by the organization as you conduct a realistic and comprehensive assessment of strengths and limitations. In general, all schools undertaking strategic planning will want to minimally include planning, assessment, implementation, and evaluation stages in their process. In other words, the school needs to identify its current status, determine what needs to improve, determine how it will improve, implement strategies to bring about change, and evaluate the results and the progress.

Information regarding strategic planning in education is limited. As stated previously, many processes in education and most of what is currently performed in schools has been adapted from business models. In researching specific approaches to strategic planning, you will see a number of models, such as the balanced scorecard and alignment planning processes that are better suited for business processes. Various models are recommended for different uses but regardless of the model selected, the planning process must be approached from a "big picture" standpoint, meaning every aspect of the organization must be scrutinized to identify the greatest needs. Information gathering is critical to a successful plan; consequently, the most up-to-date, accurate data should be secured in order to create realistic yet comprehensive strategies and action plans. The following two planning models are the most applicable to educational organizations. Each of the models has its own purpose so prior to beginning your plan you should decide which model is the more appropriate one to use for your particular situation.

Goal-Based Approach

A goal-based approach is a future-thinking approach. As a school, you will develop goals based upon your desired future state. You have already developed your mission and vision statements during the first phase of this process where you determined what you ultimately want your building to be. In this step of developing your goals to reach your desired state, often, the goals you select will be determined by federal or state requirements. Most schools will need to focus on academic goals in reading and math, so you most likely will not have much freedom here. But in selecting a third goal, you may wish to include a goal related to an area such as climate, attendance, or graduation rate. This third goal can be based on your vision of where you want your school to be several years down the road.

Once you have determined the goals, you will proceed to the collection of data in the selected areas in order to set the metrics you will include in each of the goals. In other words, you will set the measureable portion of your goals with a percentage or number of points you desire to increase based on the current level of achievement. The goal-based approach is the method most commonly used.

Issue-Based Approach

An issue based approach is a current-thinking approach. This approach operates rather indirectly from the development of the school's mission and vision. You will begin by collecting data about your building, most likely through surveys, focus groups, or discussions with members of the school community. For academic goals, you should review data from recent assessments that are available to you. Your school will determine the most important issues you are currently facing based on the data that have been gathered. From the issues that emerged as a result of the data gathering, your SPT will select the areas to be addressed in the strategic plan then create your goals. Your goals may be to increase the number of real-world learning experiences for students, increase creative writing opportunities, improve the climate of your building, or improve the daily attendance rate, for example. Data on these, as well as many other issues, can be collected from the school community for consideration. With this approach, you will create your data-gathering instruments, gather the data, and analyze the data prior to any of the goals being formulated. The issue-based approach is generally used less frequently than the goal-based approach.

Chapter Summary

The strategic planning process consists of six steps: identifying the purpose, mission, vision, and goals; collecting and analyzing data; writing the plan; implementing the plan; monitoring and evaluating progress; and revising the plan. Within each of these steps, your strategic planning team (SPT) will lead the charge along with the principal. Developing a strong SPT is important to the success of the plan and care must be taken in its formation. This chapter offers four different methods for selecting SPT members. Generally, the most effective method to use is a combination of enlisting current leadership, asking for volunteers, and appointing members.

Timelines should guide the strategic planning process. Set a timeline for the planning process of several months to a year to ensure that each phase of the process is thoroughly developed. During the planning stages, focus on several key points: keep the lines of communication open, be inclusive of all areas of the school community, make sure you have a good cross-section of staff contributing to the planning team, and seek input and feedback from the staff. Many people are resistant to change; therefore, make sure to proceed cautiously and involve staff as much as possible. Above all else, do not impose the change on the organization or else the plan will likely fail.

In terms of the approach to take in strategic planning, two are recommended. The first is a goal-based approach and the second is an issue-based approach. Both approaches are described in this chapter.

CHAPTER 3

Purpose, Mission, Vision, and Goals

Purpose

It is a forward-thinking principal who embarks upon a strategic planning process, particularly if it is a local initiative to better the school or improve achievement. At its highest level, strategic planning is undertaken to transform and revitalize your school into a high-performing team. This is the goal for which to aim. With that in mind, the organization will approach the process based on the information within the strategic plan to achieve the desired transformation. This is not a project that can be taken on single-handedly or with only a small team of members from the school. The entire school community must be aware of the opportunity and understand the need for change and the purpose of a strategic plan. It is easy for educators to become complacent or feel that they cannot make a difference. You must take steps to revitalize the staff and the culture of the school.

If you are new in a building, take some time to assess the landscape before announcing any plans to initiate changes in the school. Acknowledge the work that has been done and encourage new ideas in order to move people to think about change. This is a great time, nonetheless, to establish your role as the instructional leader and to present your vision to the school community.

As you prepare to begin the first step of this strategic planning model, take time to carefully consider then determine the purpose of the venture. The purpose must be established in order to provide direction for the planning team as well as direction for the school. The scope of the process should be broad enough to make an impact on the school but at the same time narrow enough to focus on specific goals. Therefore, a strategic planning process should encompass a limited number of areas on which to focus. Every aspect of your organization cannot be changed at one time; however, if you have a number of different areas that need to be addressed, plan to work on those you consider to be the most important first. Prioritize these areas with your planning team and decide what should go into the initial plan. A discussion of the remaining items can then assist you in determining when they should be approached in the future. Decide whether each of the areas ought to be addressed within the first three-year plan or perhaps later in a subsequent plan. Encompassing too many areas at one time will lead to frustration and could result in the plan being implemented incompletely or abandoned altogether.

In many instances, strategic planning will be conducted for the purpose of fulfilling requirements of federal or state regulations or because of requirements in grant applications. There are other times when a principal may want to conduct strategic planning efforts to provide greater direction for the school, to improve student academic achievement, or to close achievement gaps. In any case, the process will follow the same steps. Once the purpose is established, the planning team will have a clear sense of direction for the initial strategic plan. Where state or federal guidelines or grant requirements are concerned, it is vitally important to follow all guidelines as specified in order to obtain approval. If the planning process is a local endeavor, be sure to consult with the senior management of your district to acquire any approval necessary prior to initiating the process.

After considerable communication with and input from your school community, you, as the instructional leader, should frame the purpose in order to guide the planning process. As each building differs, there may be a variety of purposes for moving forward with planning, but generally speaking, the main purposes for initiating a strategic plan in your building may be to

- improve student academic achievement;
- establish a focus for the work of the school;
- improve the climate of the building;
- decrease discipline referrals;
- increase attendance and graduation rate; or
- implement new processes or programs.

The development of the statement of purpose is not a task to completely turn over to a committee or planning team, but do involve the planning team in setting the purpose and then communicating the purpose to the school community. Here is an example of a statement of purpose that could be written and shared with the school community:

City Middle School is entering into a strategic planning process beginning in November 2012. The strategic plan will be completed and ready for implementation at the beginning of the 2013-2014 school year. The purpose of the strategic planning process for City Middle School is to improve academic achievement for all students in sixth, seventh, and eighth grade reading and math, and to close the achievement gap between various demographic groups.

By now, you have thought about the prospect of strategic planning for your building and have discussed the notion with key people in the organization. Continue to expand the discussion into all areas of the school community to emphasize the need for strategic planning. In your communication, be sure to highlight the purpose in terms of the value that strategic planning can bring to the school. In addition to the stated goals you will strive to reach through the implementation of your plan, the process itself will yield additional benefits. The following figure illustrates several benefits that the strategic planning process can bring to your school along with the main benefit of increasing student academic achievement.

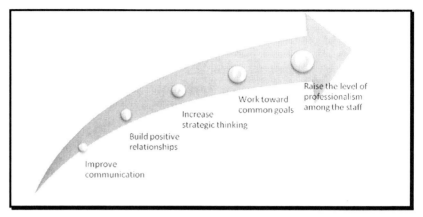

Figure 3.1. Benefits of strategic planning.

Establishing the Mission and Vision

Once the purpose has been established, the planning process must continue with identifying the organization's mission and vision. This is a step to be taken with the entire staff, not simply left to the administration or planning team. When taking on the complex task of strategic planning, a new or revised mission statement and vision statement are important to craft with your staff. The mission and vision are critical to the planning process and need to be created or, if already available, need to be reviewed and clarified prior to conducting any further steps. Many schools will already have a mission statement and a vision statement in place, especially if the school has been in existence for a long period of time. Surprisingly enough, however, you may find that the school has neither a mission statement nor a vision statement or, if such exist, have seldom been reviewed or revised. Some schools may simply use the district statements as a guide.

Establishing the mission and vision statements is a step often overlooked or quickly reviewed perhaps most often because school leaders involved in the process assume that these are already in place and generally known by all. While this may be the case, do not assume they are universally known and accepted or that they are applicable to the current circumstances. Time must still be provided to review both the mission and vision statements with the staff and to make adjustments where necessary. Embarking on the strategic planning process is the time you want everyone involved with a common framework of what drives the organization and for what the school stands. Your own versions of the mission and vision statements are essential in order to focus the attention on what is important and to bring about a shared sense of responsibility for improvement and success.

The mission and vision are many times confused with each other. The two are separate components that need to be identified independent of, yet in conjunction with, one another. Establish the mission first then craft the vision based on what you have specified in the mission statement. In its contents, the mission statement must have significant meaning to the staff. It is a concise description of the organization's overall reason for existence. The mission statement should summarize the work, provide a direction, and guide the actions of the organization. It is the school's reason for being, which should focus on a common intent.

The vision is the school's purpose in terms of what it values. A vision statement describes the future state of the organization and what the school would like to become. In other words, the vision describes where you want the school to go and what you want it to look like. The vision should challenge the staff to dream big and depict the passion of your work. A key element of successful schools is that they have a well-articulated vision that is known by everyone on the staff. Discussions of the mission and vision can generate considerable excitement and a newfound enthusiasm as staff members think broadly about the purpose of the school and what it can be in an ideal state.

Once developed, the mission and vision statements should be shared with the entire school community. The following is an example of a mission statement and a vision statement.

Mission Statement

The mission of City Middle School is to provide a caring learning environment that respects the individual needs of each student. Our staff will hold high expectations for all students and will provide rigorous, meaningful, and purposeful learning activities that engage all students.

Vision Statement

The vision of City Middle School is to be a top class educational institution that delivers high quality instruction and expects academic success for each student.

There are several ways in which to tackle the process of creating the mission and vision statements. To be fully inclusive, utilize a process that involves all members of the staff with the purpose of generating ideas from across the departments and teams. You do not want to hold a staff meeting with open discussion among the whole group as this type of process would be extremely unmanageable especially if you have a large staff. With varied thoughts and opinions of staff members, you can imagine the discussion that would occur and the lack of focus and direction of such a meeting. Rather, input can still be sought from the entire staff when generated in small groups or teams during a staff meeting or a professional development session. Plan to spend an hour to an hour and a half creating each statement separately. Once you have formulated the mission statement, the vision statement should then be created. The following section details a process that can be followed to develop your mission and vision statements.

Input must also be gathered from parents and community members, as well. With the SPT, create survey instruments that can be distributed to parents and community members. Gather as many responses as possible then analyze the data. Carefully consider the parent and community responses as the mission and vision statements are constructed.

Mission/Vision Group Process

Although a small group (the SPT) will be directly involved in the actual writing of the mission and vision statements, input must be sought from all members of the school community. When staff members are included, they truly appreciate the opportunity to offer suggestions and to know that their voices are heard. The process recommended here is best managed in a professional development session or staff meeting situation where all staff members are present. A period of about three hours, at least an hour and a half for each, is needed to complete both the mission and vision activities, so be sure to allow a sufficient amount of time. Each of the two statements should be handled separately. Two individual meeting times are best for this purpose so that each statement is approached with a fresh perspective.

To begin, staff members should be divided into small groups of six to eight people. You can assign staff members to the small groups for the purpose of arranging them together with others with whom they may not ordinarily group. A second arrangement is to situate staff members with members of their own teams or departments. The recommended arrangement is to assign the staff members to the small groups. Assigning the staff members to specific groups helps in a few different ways. First, it works to stretch their thinking. By working with people from different departments, they can hear different viewpoints and find out what issues others are experiencing. Second, assigning the staff members will provide as much diversity among the groups as possible in terms of departments, grade levels, gender, and the like. Third, staff members can begin to recognize the value others bring to the organization. Finally, you always have those people—maybe one or two—who can make group work difficult if seated together. You know who they are. This method allows you more control of the situation. Even though some may be a bit uncomfortable at first, in the long run, most people will enjoy talking with new people and they will gain a better understanding of the work done in other departments or areas. A leader for each group should be preselected and briefed on the procedures prior to the meeting in order to be able to guide the group through the process. A speaker and a recorder for each group should also be selected to handle specific responsibilities for the group as listed below.

Follow this process in developing the mission statement at the first meeting.

> ➤ Define and clarify the substance of both the mission and the vision so that everyone is clear as to what should be included in each of the statements. Outline these steps for the group prior to beginning. (10 minutes)

- ➤ Provide a set of questions to which each individual will respond in writing. (15 minutes)
- ➤ The facilitator of each group will lead a discussion of the individual responses to each of the questions. A recorder will document the common themes for each question on chart paper. (30 minutes)
- ➤ In turn, the speaker for each group will share the common themes of each question with the entire group. The main points for each question should be summarized and listed on chart paper for everyone to see. (30 minutes)
- ➤ All of the notes from this process should be collected, and from this, the SPT will formulate the first draft of the mission statement.
- ➤ Once the first draft is formulated, provide copies of the mission statement for everyone to review and make suggestions for changes.
- ➤ Once the changes are reviewed by the SPT, a final draft is written.

At a second session with the entire staff, using a set of questions pertaining to the vision statement, follow the process used for the mission statement development to create the vision statement. A detailed description of the mission and vision statement activities along with sample questions can be found in the workbook.

Communicating the Mission and Vision

Once the mission and vision are established through the group process model, the critical next step is to communicate them. The new mission and vision statements should be published on the school's website, sent home to parents in newsletters, displayed in all classrooms and common areas, shared with the community, and included in staff and parent/student handbooks. It must be clear that the mission and vision serve as the guiding factors in what drives the work of the staff and school. Activities that do not promote or align with the mission and vision should be reviewed and perhaps eliminated. Begin disseminating the mission and vision information as soon as it is in place rather than waiting until the entire strategic plan is completed. Sharing the information once it is prepared will prove beneficial for several reasons.

- ➤ The direction for the school will be set.
- ➤ The school community will be aware of the focus.
- ➤ A sense of collegiality will develop.
- ➤ The notion of shared responsibility for results will pervade.
- ➤ The entire school community—staff, students, parents, and community—will know you are ready to embark on planned improvement strategies.

Goals

There are, in general, two times within the strategic planning process where goal setting can be conducted: prior to or following the data-gathering phase. You may want to know how it is possible to set goals prior to data gathering, seeing as how this is a data-driven process, when you have not yet collected any data. Think back to chapter 2 and the discussion on the goal-based approach and the issue-based approach to goal setting. The data gathering occurs at different times based on the approach you decide to utilize.

As mentioned earlier, you may be involved in the strategic planning process based on outside requirements, such as improving reading and math scores based on federal guidelines. Following this scenario, you already know the areas on which you need to focus (goal-based approach) because of the federal requirements. For your third goal, you may already know that you want to improve the climate of the building, for example, based on building concerns.

On the other hand, you may want to wait until data are gathered and analyzed to identify critical areas of need in order to truly create a data-driven process. In this case, you will base your decision on the individual needs (issue-based approach) discovered through analysis of the data you collect on a variety of issues. For example, you may decide to survey the staff to determine what they believe are the most pressing issues. Once survey data are reviewed, you will have clear evidence of the areas that need to be addressed.

Typically, a school should set three to five goals. Attempting to tackle more issues in one plan can become too much to maintain and may therefore become overwhelming.

Goal Setting Prior to Data Collection

When setting your goals prior to data collection, you are conducting a goal-based approach to strategic planning. The goals you set will be broad and overarching. The manner in which you reach these goals, however, will be developed in depth in later steps. The purpose for setting goals at this point is to identify where your data gathering needs to occur. Continuing with the example of improving the climate of the building, you will create a goal that can be measured at a point in time prior to beginning the improvement strategies. Once the strategies have been implemented, the metrics will be measured again at predetermined points that will be stated in your action plan. Your goal may be, for example, to decrease the number of discipline referrals to the office. Your strategies and action steps will be developed around this goal. This is a true goal-based approach since you are setting the goals, gathering baseline data with which to compare future data, and then implementing strategies and action steps to achieve those goals.

Goal Setting After Data Collection

Choosing to collect data prior to goal setting follows an issue-based approach, which can provide a clear picture of the areas of need in your building. If you are following this approach, you are proactively utilizing data to make decisions. In other words, you see the need to think and plan strategically and you are not being "forced" into creating a plan or making improvements in certain areas in your building, but you are being guided by what the data show. Once you gather the data, work with your SPT to analyze the data and identify areas for improvement. Again, your goal may be to reduce the number of discipline referrals to the office. However, since gathering data before setting the goal, you found, for example, that discipline referrals to the office are originating from one particular grade level. In this case, there would be no need to create a goal to decrease the number of discipline referrals for the whole school, but since you have pinpointed the source, you can write your goal to target that particular grade level. This is considered to be an issue-based approach since you are collecting data to see what issues emerge then creating your goals based on the data.

SMART Goals

Whether setting goals prior to or following the data collection step, you want to state your goals in a meaningful way. You can accomplish this by developing SMART goals. You have, no doubt, heard of SMART goals. SMART is an acronym for

Specific

Measurable

Attainable

Realistic

Timely

While there are variations for the terms in the acronym, for instance, the R could stand for realistic, relevant, reasonable, or results-oriented, the words applied here are most commonly used. You can substitute other words to assist your team in understanding the concept. When creating SMART goals, there are key points to remember for each step. The following is a description of each of the areas required within the SMART goals.

Specific—the goal should be well defined and clearly understood by anyone reading it. A specifically stated goal will help you determine if, in fact, you reach the goal when you clearly state how much of an increase is desired.

Measureable—by including a metric by which to judge the results, you will be able to easily identify whether or not you have made the progress you desire. Stating that you will improve the passage rate of third graders in reading by 20 percent, for example, is something that can be measured. Using the most recent passage rate, compute 20 percent of the score; add it to the current passage rate to get the new passage rate goal. As an example, this year's passage rate was 62 percent, 20 percent of which equals 12.4 percent. Add that to 62 percent and the passage rate goal for the new year will be 74.4 percent.

Attainable—set the goal to an amount that is not within an easy reach, but within a "stretch." Set a practical goal, but not one that will set you up for failure. Many times, goals are set to reflect a 10 percent or 20 percent increase from the current score, which will most generally be reachable.

Realistic—this is where a good, honest assessment is necessary. Given your current circumstances, consider the availability of resources and where you stand compared to the standard you need to attain.

Time Bound—the goal should be time specific. Include a set amount of time so that everyone is aware of what needs to be accomplished by when and has the sense of urgency to get the job done.

Typically, you will set three goals. Attempting more than three goals becomes unmanageable and difficult to monitor. In the long run, frustration will set in as you attempt to "fix" everything at once. Fewer than three goals can be created, but while you are involved in this major undertaking, you might as well maximize your efforts and incorporate goals in the major areas. Generally, it is recommended that you construct two academic goals, one in reading and one in math, and one nonacademic goal, such as a goal related to climate or attendance. In covering these three areas, everyone within the organization will be involved to some extent in working to achieve the goals.

Educators are usually well-versed in writing goals; however, including all of the elements in a SMART goal can take some practice. The following are three examples of goals along with the goal rewritten in the SMART format. You and your SPT should try your hand at writing each of the three goals in the SMART format before looking at the examples. Remember to construct goals that are specific, measurable, attainable, realistic, and time bound. Divide the SPT into three groups: one for math, one for reading, and one for climate. Members of the team should select the academic or nonacademic goal group in which they would like to participate. The selection should be made based on expertise or interest in the particular area. Once assigned to a goal group, the SPT members should remain on the selected goal to ensure continuity throughout the entire process. Review each of the goals below.

Goal 1

All students will show evidence of one year of growth in mathematics.

Goal 1 written as a SMART goal:

During the 2008-2009 school year, 90 percent of the seventh-grade students will improve their math achievement scores as measured by a one-year gain in national grade equivalent compared to the 2007-2008 math problem solving subtest.

An analysis of this goal indicates that it is a SMART goal.

Specific—The area is math achievement.
Measurable—The amount of growth is a one-year gain.
Attainable—Seventh-graders should be prepared to reach this goal.
Realistic—It may be a stretch, but perhaps possible, to have 90 percent of all seventh-grade students improve by a grade equivalent of one year.
Time bound—At the end of the 2008-2009 school year, results from 2008 to 2009 are to be compared with results from 2007 to 2008.

Goal 2

Students will improve their reading comprehension skills on the district reading assessment.

Goal 2 written as a SMART goal:

Ninety percent of third-grade students will demonstrate reading proficiency by earning a score of 75 percent or higher as measured by the district reading assessment administered at the end of third grade.

An analysis of this goal indicates that it is a SMART goal:

Specific—The area is reading comprehension.
Measurable—Students will earn a score of 75 percent or higher.
Attainable—All third graders should be able to read at a proficient level.
Realistic—It is reasonable to expect that 90 percent of the students could reach this goal.
Time bound—Students will reach this by the end of third grade.

Goal 3

Decrease the number of discipline referrals to the office.

Goal 3 written as a SMART goal:

The number of discipline referrals to the office will decrease 20 percent during the second quarter of the 2007-2008 school year as compared to discipline referral data for the second quarter of the 2006-2007 school year.

An analysis of this goal indicates that it is a SMART goal.

Specific—The number of office referrals.
Measurable—A 20 percent decrease.
Attainable—A 20 percent decrease is a moderate amount.
Realistic—A school could expect this type of decrease, given the new strategies that will be implemented.
Time bound—Data from the second quarter of the current year are compared to the same time period of the previous year.

After practicing with these examples, the SPT should practice writing SMART goals for your own school goals.

Creating SMART goals will provide a solid base on which to build the strategies and action plans. Your goals should be created to reflect the mission and vision you have established for your school. Your goals should encompass the entire three-year timeframe of your strategic plan; therefore, you should consider writing an incremental goal. A goal written incrementally would be, for example, to increase the passage rate by 10 percent each year for the three years of the plan. If your school has a long way to go to reach the desired gains, aim for a higher goal.

Chapter Summary

Strategic planning can be carried out for a number of reasons, but most of all, utilizing a strategic planning process will demonstrate your commitment to school improvement. You will find that there are additional benefits that will result from your efforts. Improved communication, improved working relationships, and strategic thinking are a few examples of positive changes you may see. Communication remains an important element in this step of the plan.

Schools may or may not already have a mission statement and a vision statement. If the statements exist, they need to be thoroughly examined and perhaps revised as you begin this process. If no such documents exist, you will need to work with the staff to create original statements. A group process for establishing the mission and vision statements is included in this chapter.

Goal setting follows the creation of the mission and vision statements and can be completed prior to or after data collection, depending on the approach you utilize. SMART goals will help you and your team establish the outcomes you desire and will result in clearly defined goals that will set the expectations for your staff. The SMART goal format provides the direction needed as you write specific, measurable, attainable, realistic, and timely goals.

CHAPTER 4

Data Collection and Analysis

Data-driven decisions are essential in today's educational climate. Data are required to identify your strengths and to identify your areas of need. Prior to setting the goals or once the goals are identified, depending on the method used, the assessment of the current state of the school will be the guide for the strategies and action plans to come. You may already know or have an idea of where improvements need to take place in your building but backing up the ideas with data supplies an objective view of the situation. Using data leads to better decision making. In times prior to focusing on data within the planning process, administrators and teachers relied on intuition, thoughts, or feelings to address what they believed to be the needs of the school. There were no measurements to show whether or not improvements were made. With a data-driven approach, clearly identified areas for improvement can be targeted.

The following figure illustrates the differences between traditional decision making used in the past and data-driven decision making used today.

Decision Making Comparison Chart

Traditional Decision Making	Data-Driven Decision Making
Parent communication details activities and events through newsletters and open houses.	Parent communication details student progress.
Budget decisions are based on prior practice or priority programs.	Budget allocations are focused on identified needs.
A one-size-fits-all staff development is provided.	Focused professional development is provided to address documented areas of need.
Reports to the school community provide information regarding school events and programs.	Factual reports to the school community state the learning progress of students.
Goal setting is top down.	Goal setting is based on an analysis of needs.
Staff meetings are focused on operations and the dissemination of information.	Staff meetings are focused on issues raised by the data.

Figure 4.1. Decision making comparison chart.

Data gathering takes many forms and originates from multiple sources. Data will need to be gathered from informational sources, such as test scores, grades, and attendance, and from groups of individuals, such as parents, students, teachers, staff, and community members. Without going into detail on statistical data, those working on the SPT should know in general the two types of data to be gathered: quantitative data and qualitative data. Quantitative data are derived from sources, such as test scores, grades, and attendance. These data may be obtained from a variety of grade levels and over several years at each grade level in order to provide good, comparative data. The more comparative data available, the better the analysis will be as you will then be able to look at trends at particular grade levels, in specific subject areas, or for individual students. The SPT can search out trends or patterns in the data during the analysis stage that may provide detail as to the areas in greatest need of improvement and where resources should be allocated. Quantitative data can be compared from one year to the next or from one grade level to another. The data should provide as much information as possible about the students, student learning, and the school as a whole, particularly if climate issues are to be addressed in the strategic planning process.

Qualitative data are derived from sources, such as surveys, focus groups, and interviews that can be conducted with various constituencies of the school. Qualitative data provide anecdotal information regarding a range of programs, policies, or processes. These data will provide insight into beliefs and ideas of the constituencies. Survey, interview, or focus group questions should be developed to cover multiple facets of the school. Qualitative data can create a picture of the current state of the building from a variety of perspectives. Quantitative and qualitative data are necessary for a well-planned and purposeful process and can be categorized into four areas as illustrated in figure 4.2 below.

Quantitative and Qualitative Data Sources

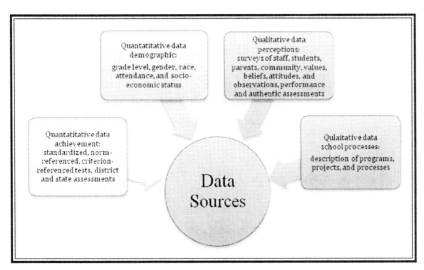

Figure 4.2. Achievement, demographic, perception, and school processes data sources.

Achievement Data

Where academic goals are concerned, such as increasing achievement scores in reading and math, past achievement data for individual students is critical to collect. An assessment of individual students' skills can determine their needs. Identifying students' current levels of performance and working with students individually are critical pieces in this strategic planning model, which will be discussed in chapter 5 on writing the strategic plan. Therefore, collecting individual student data on each of the content standards tested supplies crucial information. You will then be able to make decisions regarding the strategies or interventions needed to achieve the desired improvements for each individual student.

Teachers must know their students' levels of performance in all content areas in order to be able to objectively determine their needs and areas for improvement. These data, though, come from a number of sources. You cannot solely rely on standardized test data or state achievement data. A tiered approach should be implemented that will serve to encompass several levels or layers of data that are collected at various times and in varied amounts throughout the year. These together will provide a complete and comprehensive representation of student academic achievement, which will be necessary when writing the action plans into the strategic planning document. A record of the student information—referred to as the status report—should be maintained by classroom teachers. The status report is a valuable document which contains student information that is used for the purpose of monitoring progress. Status reports will be discussed in chapter 7.

As an example of tiered assessments, figure 4.3 illustrates three tiers of assessment data that may be utilized.

Tiered Assessments

Level	Frequency	Type
Federal/State	Annually	State achievement assessments Norm-referenced tests Criterion-referenced tests
District	Quarterly	District required assessments
School/Classroom	Ongoing	Teacher-made tests Short-cycle assessments Teacher observations

Figure 4.3. Tiered assessment data.

The most useful of all of these data are the ongoing assessments at the school and classroom level because they provide the most current data if properly written and administered. Classroom assessments should be modeled after state assessments in order to mine the most accurate and useful information possible to assist teachers in making decisions about their instruction. For example, if your state assessment contains constructed response questions where students are required to write out their answers rather than bubble in a multiple-choice response, classroom teachers must create comparable questions to use in daily lessons. Questions should include the structure and vocabulary students will see on the actual test. Practical applications of questions that mirror those on the state assessment should be presented to students for practice as part of the daily lessons in the reading and math as well as other content areas tested. Providing practice on these types of questions will not only present students with a model of what to expect on the test but will also supply valuable information to the teachers as to the students' needs for intervention or assistance.

As previously discussed, it is important to utilize multiple sources of data in the strategic planning process. In the example of improving math problem-solving skills, relying on annual state assessment data or yearly standardized test data are not adequate measures. You will need additional local formative assessment data gathered throughout the year to determine whether or not students are on track to make the desired gains. These additional measures should be determined by the SPT with input from subject area teachers.

Along with establishing student needs through data analysis, you also need to identify staff needs in terms of understanding and interpreting the data presented. Appropriate here is a discussion of expanding teachers' knowledge of data. Many teachers have an aversion to the topic of data and data analysis; however, it is imperative that teachers know how to read standardized test reports and state assessment data and possess a good understanding of the terms used in federal guidelines and state report card information. Terms such as "adequate yearly progress" (AYP), percentile rank, and item analysis are just a few examples of the terminology that teachers should be familiar with related to reading the testing and assessment information. Do not assume that teachers know how to read and interpret the data. Many teachers do not have experience in this area. Special sessions held during regular staff meetings or subject area meetings should be conducted to instruct teachers in the basics of data analysis and interpretation.

SWOT Analysis

A data analysis technique utilized regularly in business applications is the SWOT analysis. This technique evaluates the organization's strengths, weaknesses, opportunities, and threats (SWOT) and is typically completed in a matrix format. In the educational setting, the strengths and weaknesses are generally internal factors, such as content knowledge of the teachers or student participation, and the opportunities and threats are generally external factors, such as funding or resources. This technique may be applied in your setting if you choose and can be used as an additional tool to gather data. The data will provide a baseline to which future data-gathering initiatives will be compared in order to identify whether or not growth has occurred. This type of analysis can pinpoint areas for improvement as you work to reduce the weaknesses and minimize the threats within your organization. The SWOT analysis is mentioned only briefly here because it may be best utilized in the business world where external factors, in particular, are relied on more heavily. This is one example of the many data analysis techniques available.

SWOT Analysis

Strengths	Weaknesses
Opportunities	Threats

Figure 4.4. SWOT analysis chart.

Gap Analysis

Once data are gathered, a thorough analysis should be conducted to determine the direction your strategic plan will take. You want to identify not only areas for improvement but also the extent to which improvement needs to occur. To determine the difference between the current state and the desired state, a gap analysis should be conducted. A gap analysis compares the current performance with the potential performance. In other words, a gap analysis evaluates the difference in where you are at the present time with where you want to be at a given time in the future. It compares the projected scope and degree of the problem with the existing resources that are currently in place to determine what needs to occur. Pinpoint the desired end state and then, through use of the data you gathered, identify the current state. You will then look at the difference between the two. The comparison between the current state and the desired results will show where gaps lie and the extent to which the gap exists.

Also important to conduct are gap analyses of the existing differences among all demographic areas. These are the specific areas, according to federal guidelines, where growth needs to be shown. In the educational setting, the gap analysis typically identifies the difference in test scores, for example, between various socioeconomic groups or racial groups when compared to one another. You will also be able to see the current achievement levels of each of the demographic groups compared to the desired achievement levels for each group. So you will not only compare the groups to each other but will also compare each group to the standard that needs to be achieved. Given these data, the SPT will need to establish the targets for each of the goals that have already been identified if you are following a goals-based approach. Metrics should be set for each of the individual demographic groups so that the goals can be defined for each. In the case of an issues-based plan, your data will reveal the areas of greatest need and show the difference between the current condition and the desired state when comparing the various demographic groups to one another as well as comparing the demographic groups to the standard. The challenge then is to determine the strategies that are needed to close the gaps. To illustrate, consider the following examples.

The first example illustrates the gap in baseline data compared to the standard.

> Assume that you want to improve math achievement scores for tenth-graders on the state assessment by 25 percent over the three years of the plan. Your current pass rate is 60 percent. A 25 percent increase will result in a fifteen-point gain to a pass rate of 75 percent. To accomplish this over a three-year period, the improvement needed in each of the three years is five percentage points. The goal for the first year would be a 65 percent pass rate, the goal for the second year would be a 70 percent pass rate, and the goal for the third year would be a 75 percent pass rate.

The graph below displays the math achievement goal data for the current school year and the three years of the strategic plan as stated in the example. The graph indicates the pass rate percentage needed each year to achieve the final goal of a 75 percent pass rate by end of the 2016 school year.

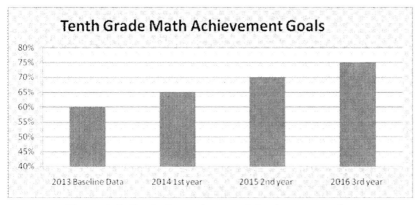

Figure 4.5. Goals for each year of the three-year plan
compared to the baseline data.

The second example illustrates socioeconomic levels compared to the standard and compared to each other.

With a pass rate of 40 percent, the low socioeconomic group has a difference or gap of 35 percentage points when comparing the pass rate to the standard. With a pass rate of 62 percent, the high socioeconomic group has a difference or gap of 13 percentage points when comparing the pass rate to the standard. When comparing the groups to the standard, this example shows that both groups posted a pass rate that is below the standard. When comparing the groups to each other, the high socioeconomic group, while failing to meet the standard, posted a pass rate that is 22 percentage points higher than the low socioeconomic group. Therefore, the difference or gap between the low socioeconomic group and the high socioeconomic group is 22 percentage points.

The graph below displays the achievement level of the low socioeconomic group and the high socioeconomic group compared to the standard to be achieved. The graph indicates that while the high socioeconomic group posted a higher pass rate than the low socioeconomic group, both groups still fell below the standard.

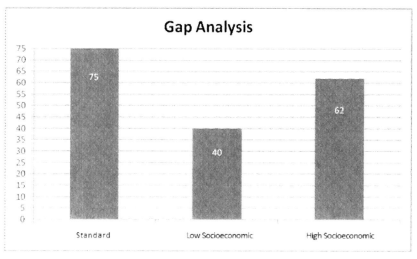

Figure 4.6. The comparison of low socioeconomic
to high socioeconomic students.

While these are illustrated in very basic terms, the first example displays the targets for the three-year period. Keep in mind that the goals can be adjusted during the predetermined reviews and the targets can be revised as necessary. If the result at the end of the first year is 70 percent, you could elect to increase the goal for the second and third years. This is something that is decided upon in the revision phase of the plan.

The second example illustrates the state standard of a 75 percent pass rate along with the current data from the demographic category of low socioeconomic students and high socioeconomic students. With the gaps identified, teachers then need to determine the instructional strategies and intervention methods to employ with each of the groups.

As with all other aspects of the strategic plan, make certain there is a good understanding on the part of your staff members as to the meaning behind the gap analysis. The identification of existing gaps does not place fault or blame, rather it serves as a method of examining current conditions and factors that contribute to the current state. Once gaps are identified, the SPT and the teachers can begin to develop strategies to address the issues. Strategies for each of the groups in the examples above may need to be varied. The details of the strategies will be delineated in the action steps within the action plan portion of the strategic plan. Teachers will need to identify the students that fall into each category in order to tailor the strategies to individual students' needs.

Frequency Table and Frequency Distribution

The quality of the data you collect should be thoroughly reviewed before they are used in any type of analysis. You want to be sure you have collected complete data to analyze. If, for example, you will utilize fifth-grade math achievement scores as your current state, you must be certain that you have as close to 100 percent of the students' scores, or scores of all students tested, available to you. The data can tell a very different story if a large number of scores is missing. In addition, the data should be reviewed in a variety of ways. One of the most common types of analysis is a frequency distribution. A frequency distribution takes a look at every score reported and counts the number of times each variable or score is reported. The following example illustrates a frequency distribution chart.

The state assessment scores shown below were reported for Mrs. Smith's fifth-grade math class. The scores ranged from 365 to 450 in increments of five points. A score of 400 was needed to pass. There are thirty students in the class.

395	405	395	415	400
415	395	420	395	415
400	405	395	400	385
450	410	410	390	365
405	400	395	405	390
410	390	400	395	390

Figure 4.7. State assessment scores for Mrs. Smith's fifth-grade class.

Looking at the set of scores above means little unless you have an organized manner in which to arrange the data. A frequency table is a tool that can be used to assist in analyzing the students' scores. It is a visual representation that states the values, or scores, and how often each of the values (scores) occurred. The frequency table allows you to visually view and interpret the data more easily in a meaningful way.

Score	Frequency
365	1
370	0
380	0
385	1
390	4
395	7
400	5
405	4
410	3
415	3
420	1
425	0
430	0
435	0
440	0
445	0
450	1

Figure 4.8. Frequency table.

The frequency table lists each of the values from lowest to highest. The lowest score was 365 and the highest score was 450. Notice that the values of all scores between 365 and 450 are listed, even though no one received some of the scores, in order to show the full range. The scores with zero frequency are necessary if further statistical data will be reported. For the purposes of this example, the frequency table with the frequency distribution is shown. The frequency of each score in figure 4.8 is determined simply by counting the number of times each score appears in the data set from figure 4.7.

In the frequency table example above, Mrs. Smith should list the student names beside each of the scores for her own use so she will know who the scores represent. The scores alone are helpful to know, but beyond that, knowing who achieved each of the scores provides a complete picture for the classroom teacher. With this additional information, Mrs. Smith can make sound instructional decisions for her students.

What information can be mined from the frequency table? The following are examples: the highest score, the lowest score, the number of students who scored at or above the passing score of 400, the number of students who scored below the passing score of 400, the percentage of students who passed, the percentage of students who failed, the number of students who failed by a small margin, the number of students who failed by a large margin, and so on. Strategies will need to be written to address students who scored well below the passing score as well as those who scored near the passing score. You can imagine that strategies will be different for the student who scores 365 than for a student who scores a 395. In the individual classrooms, teachers will need to compile a list of the names of students along with the score for each of those students in order to determine the appropriate strategies required to meet the individual students' needs.

Other measures that are helpful in analyzing data are descriptive statistics, which are measures of central tendency, including mean, median, and mode. The mean is the mathematical average of a set of numbers or scores. The median is the score located at the center of a list of all of the scores. The mode is the most frequently occurring score in a set of scores. Using the data set above in figure 4.8, the mean is 401, the median is 400, and the mode is 395.

You not only need scores but also need to know the specific areas within the content where students are low. From there, you can determine the strategies that will best address the weaknesses. With a good understanding of these basic data collection and data analysis tools, you will be able to readily determine the needs of your students. You and your team will be able to make the best data-driven decisions possible. In addition, a good understanding of these tools is necessary when it comes to the monitoring and evaluation phase of the plan.

Item Analysis

Item analysis is another data analysis technique that is extremely beneficial to classroom teachers. There are a couple of definitions of and uses for this term. Item analysis can be used by teachers or test writers to assess the quality of test items. It may be used to improve the teacher's or test writer's ability to construct test items. Teachers can use item analysis to judge how difficult or how easy a test item seemed to be for a class. When a teacher observes that a large number of students missed a particular question, he or she will know that more time should be spent on that content or that the test item may not have been written clearly.

Item analysis is used here as a means of examining student responses to multiple choice test items rather than reviewing the items themselves. As an example, shown in the figure below are five multiple choice items with four possible answer choices from which to select. Fifty students responded to each of the five items. The figure shows the item number and the number of students who selected each of the answer choices A, B, C, or D. The correct response for each item is the bolded number.

Item Number	Response A	Response B	Response C	Response D
1	8	**30**	4	8
2	**40**	0	3	7
3	15	6	14	**15**
4	0	5	**38**	7
5	9	12	**13**	16

Figure 4.9 Item analysis

There is a great deal of information a teacher can gather from this item analysis table. Thirty students selected the correct response B, for item one. Forty students selected the correct response A, for item two. Thirty-eight students selected the correct response C, for item four. It could be said that the class did fairly well on item one (60% answered correctly), quite well on item two (80% answered correctly), and fairly well on item four (76% answered correctly).

Results were very different for items three and five. Only fifteen students (30%), answered item three correctly. The same number of students selected A as their answer choice, fourteen students selected C as their answer choice, and six selected B as their answer choice. Notice that thirty-five students (70%) answered the item incorrectly. Only thirteen students (26%), answered item five correctly and thirty-seven students (74%) answered it incorrectly. More students answered these two items incorrectly compared to the number of students who answered them correctly.

A teacher can find valuable information from this short example. Items three and five may have been unclear or perhaps these concepts were not emphasized enough in the instruction. A teacher should look at the responses in each of these items to find out what may have caused the students to select the wrong answers. It is also helpful for the teacher to talk with the students after the test to find out why they answered as they did.

Encourage teachers to make use of the item analysis technique. It can help pinpoint areas in need of reteaching and it can show the teacher where intervention needs to occur. Along with making general statements about the number of students who answered incorrectly, by looking deeper at each student's test, teachers can list those students by name that missed specific items and can provide the assistance needed. An item analysis from state assessments should be evaluated, but in addition, teachers should also evaluate item analysis reports for district assessments and classroom tests. The data will reveal strengths and weaknesses in specific areas of the content which teachers can then address.

Chapter Summary

Many teachers find the topic of data analysis to be daunting and sometimes intimidating, but in education today, accountability requires that we accept and embrace it. Data-driven decisions must be made instead of relying on traditional decisions that stemmed from what educators thought or felt was needed.

Just a few basics of data analysis will allow teachers to be able to determine students' needs and to set goals accordingly. The concept of a gap analysis is presented and explained. It is necessary for teachers to be able to identify gaps in achievement whether it is the whole class related to a standard or one demographic group compared to another.

A general understanding of quantitative and qualitative data is needed. Quantitative data can come from standardized assessments, classroom assessments, or demographic information, to name a few. Qualitative data can come from sources such as surveys, observations, or descriptions of programs.

A frequency distribution supplies the teacher with a visual representation of a list of scores, such as test scores, and displays them in an easy-to-use format. Frequency distribution is another data analysis tool with which teachers should be familiar. A great deal of information can be derived from a few basic data analysis techniques.

An item analysis is useful in identifying strengths and weaknesses in specific areas of the content. It can assist teachers in focusing their instruction and intervention.

CHAPTER 5

Writing the Plan

A good strategic plan should delineate exactly how your school's goals will be met. Each of the goals should have a set of strategies listed including action steps that detail precisely what is to be done, who is responsible, resources needed, the timeframe, and the evidence required to indicate whether or not the strategy was successful. This document is called the Action Plan. An action plan is developed for each of the goals in your plan, and once finalized, a copy should be provided to each member of the staff and to selected members of the school community. The plan will provide the detail as to the manner in which each of the goals is to be achieved. The entire strategic plan will consist of several pages including a cover page, a list of the SPT members, the mission and vision page, the goals page, and the action plan pages. The workbook contains a template for each section of the strategic planning document as well as information and directions for completing the plan and for conducting many of the professional development activities.

Goal Setting

The topic of writing goals was presented in chapter 3; however, it must be noted that setting the actual metrics within the school goals is another area that may prompt serious discussion. There are different schools of thought on the topic regarding the amount of growth that should be expected to be accomplished. As a moderate improvement goal, some may take the approach of looking for a 10 percent gain in the achievement levels for an academic area which is considered an incremental increase. To illustrate this example, consider a state where the standard to be met is a 75 percent pass rate, meaning 75 percent of the students need to pass the assessment in order for the school to meet the standard. A school that achieved a pass rate of 60 percent on the eighth-grade math state assessment would need to achieve a pass rate of 66 percent the next year to meet the goal of a 10 percent improvement. This incremental goal would be realistic for this situation. This school would reach its goal of a 75 percent pass rate the third year of the plan, provided that the goals were met each year. On the other hand, a school may opt to go for a loftier goal. For example, a school that achieved a pass rate of 30 percent on the eighth-grade math state assessment would need to reach 33 percent the following year to achieve a 10 percent growth. A 10 percent growth for this school would result in a very minimal gain. This school should want to set a much higher goal because, in this example, the pass rate is so far below the mark that it needs to aggressively work to improve the results.

In the business setting, organizations employ what are known as breakthrough strategies for improvement. Breakthrough strategies include, among other areas, visioning and action planning, and are necessary if the gap you need to close is large. If this is the case in your school, you must utilize strategies that will produce high-impact results. Using the previous examples, the second school illustrated produced results that are forty-five percentage points below the standard. By making incremental improvements, for example, the second school would take ten years to reach its goal of a 75 percent pass rate, provided that the goals were met each year. This school cannot afford to operate on the incremental improvement strategy. Swift and serious improvement is necessary. The school must aggressively set the goals to be attained and employ specific, rigorous action steps to get results. The higher the goals are set, the higher the levels of achievement will be. Setting your expectations and your goals higher will prompt a greater sense of urgency among the staff to achieve greater results. The staff will respond to the challenge when provided the appropriate skills and knowledge. Making use of a proactive rather than a reactive approach will bring about the desired changes. Hold high expectations for all staff. The staff should hold higher expectations for individual student progress as well.

The Strategic Plan

You are now ready to create your written plan. You have set your goals and have completed the data collection and analysis. You have gathered, and will continue to gather, input from subject area teachers regarding implementation strategies. The SPT members are now ready to convene for a productive session as they prepare to begin the hard work of developing the strategies and details that will become the road map over the course of the next three years. While the entire strategic planning process is time consuming, a considerable amount of time and energy should be placed on the writing of the action plans. Working with the SPT as a whole group, review the goals for your plan. Spend adequate time working with the group on how to write effective strategies. Details are extremely important here as you want to be certain the strategies are clear, concise, and easy to understand by those responsible for the implementation. Create a numbering system for the strategies and action steps to provide an easy method of identification. For example, the first reading strategy could be numbered 1.1. Each of the action steps, resources, persons responsible, etc., will be numbered 1.1a, 1.1b, 1.1c, and so on to relate back to the first strategy. The sample action plan in figure 5.7 illustrates the numbering concept. Remember that you want to be sure to gather ideas and input from subject area teachers for the academic goals and from staff responsible for the nonacademic goals. Bringing in ad hoc committee members at this point for specific content area expertise is advisable.

Set aside time during an SPT meeting solely for the purpose of discussing strategy writing and for practicing the writing of implementation strategies. It is not easy to write complete strategies and detailed action steps, but some practice will assist the group in feeling more comfortable with including all that is necessary in the steps. In addition, be sure to share sample strategies to model the format and content. Once you and the SPT are at ease with strategy writing, divide the team into three groups to begin writing the strategies. Using the previous examples, there will be a reading goals group, a math goals group, and a climate goals group. SPT members will again select one group in which to participate, based on expertise or interest. The SPT members should remain in the same groups as previously divided for all writing activities, if possible. Try to provide three separate locations for the goals groups to meet so that their focus and attention are on their own individual goal. One member in each group should serve as the facilitator for the writing process. Another member of the group should serve as the writer. You, as the instructional leader, should move from group to group to respond to questions, supply input, and observe each group's process. The groups should schedule additional meeting time as necessary to complete the writing of their action plans.

The SPT should be sure to address these key points as they prepare to write the plan:

> Schedule SPT meetings at predetermined times to complete the writing of the plan.
> Break down the tasks by assigning each of the goals to smaller subgroups within the SPT (for example, three goals, divide into three groups).
> Select a lead person for each of the subgroups to facilitate and keep each group on track.
> Select a writer for each group to record all information.
> Allocate sufficient resources to provide for complete implementation of the strategies.
> Gather information and ideas from those who will be implementing strategies for each goal in order to create effective action plans.
> Create a numbering system for each of the goals and strategies for ease of identification.

Figure 5.1. Key points to remember in writing the strategic plan.

A sample and description of each section is shown here.

➤ Cover page: List the name of the school, the title of the document, the date completed, and the school years in which the document will be in effect. Figure 5.2 illustrates the cover page.

City Middle School

Three-Year Strategic Plan
for

2010-2011, 2011-2012, 2012-2013

Approved: May 30, 2010

Figure 5.2. Strategic plan cover page.

➤ Lists the members of the SPT. It is a good idea to include the list of members for two reasons:

1. so that people who are serving on the team will be recognized
2. so that people in the organization know who they can contact with questions or comments about the plan

City Middle School
Strategic Planning Team

Principal   Counselor
Assistant principal   Math teacher
Reading teacher   Math teacher
Reading teacher   Secretary
Instructional assistant   Parent
Attendance officer   PE teacher
Intervention specialist   Parent
Students

Figure 5.3. Strategic planning team members.

➤ Mission and vision page: This section is self-explanatory; place a copy of the school's mission and vision statements, which you have just recently created or updated, on this page. Figure 5.4 illustrates the mission and vision page.

City Middle School
Mission and Vision Statements

Mission	Vision
The mission of City Middle School is to provide a caring learning environment that respects the individual needs of each student. Our staff will hold high expectations for all students and will provide rigorous, meaningful, and purposeful learning activities that engage all students.	The vision of City Middle School is to be a top class educational institution that delivers high-quality instruction and expects educational success for each student.

Figure 5.4. Mission and vision statement page.

➢ Goals page: On this document, state the school's formal goals, written in SMART goal format. Figure 5.5 illustrates the goals page.

City Middle School Strategic Plan
2011-2013
Goals

Goal 1: Math
The eighth-grade math scores on the state achievement assessment will increase by 10 percent each year of the three-year plan.

Goal 2: Reading
Of the 145 eighth-grade students, 90 percent will achieve a passing score on the state achievement test at the end of the 2012-2013 school year.

Goal 3: Climate
Discipline referrals to the office will decrease by 20 percent each quarter of the 2012-2013 school year as compared to each quarter of the 2011-2012 school year.

Figure 5.5. Strategic plan goals page.

➢ Action plan pages: Begin a new set of action plan pages for each of the goals. Specific details need to be included in this section in order to ensure each of the strategies is carried out properly. Figure 5.6 illustrates the action plan strategies page.

Strategies	Implemen- tation Steps	Resources Needed	Person(s) Responsible	Evaluation / Indicators of Success	Timeline

Figure 5.6. Action plan page.

Your strategic plan is initially written to encompass the entire three-year period (or the length you determine) of the plan. As the SPT convenes again to conduct the actual writing of the action plans, divide the team into the three work groups as previously divided, one group for each of the three goals in your plan. For each of your goals, you will begin a new set of strategies pages. Keep in mind that you want to create strategies within your action plan that can be accomplished in the timeframe stated. Not all strategies can be implemented at once; some strategies may not begin until the second or even the third year of the plan and should be stated as such. The more specific you can be with your strategies and especially with how the strategies will be implemented through the action steps, the better your plan will be. For example, if six different math teachers are responsible for implementing a particular math strategy, you want everyone implementing the strategy in the same manner. Detail each strategy as specifically as possible to ensure fidelity of implementation.

Strategy Writing

How does the SPT go about writing effective strategies? What will be different this time that will bring about the desired changes? To answer these questions, refer to the discussions on the various phases in this strategic planning process. The common link throughout every phase was communication. Communication is a major consideration in strategy writing, as well. The SPT, with input from appropriate staff members, will write the strategies for the building level plan. From there, each teacher creates his or her classroom level plan. Along with good communication about the strategies, professional development must be included to ensure teachers are able to implement the strategies as desired and monitoring the use of the selected strategies must be carried out.

Let's look at the building level plan first. The building level plan will state the strategies in a general framework. It will delineate the strategies and generally stated action plans, but will allow teachers to indicate the specific action steps to be carried out in their classroom level plans. Therefore to create the building strategies, the SPT will identify the needs through data gathering and analysis then identify strategies that will best suit the needs. Research-based strategies, such as those promoted by Marzano, should be utilized. Strategies that are supported by research and are proven to be effective will assist in meeting the goals you have set. As an example, one of Marzano's strategies, non-linguistic representations, has been shown to produce a 27 percentile gain in achievement. The SPT may incorporate this strategy in the action plan. The implementation step may indicate that teachers will make use of graphic organizers in their classrooms.

When creating the classroom level plans, teachers will incorporate non-linguistic representations as a strategy. When detailing the implementation steps, teachers will specifically state the type of graphic organizers they will use and how they will use them. Teachers may select a particular type of graphic organizer, such as the descriptive organizer, for a specific group of students. Other students may utilize another type of graphic organizer, such as the concept organizer. A teacher may select a certain type of organizer based on the interest or ability level of the students or provide a list of organizers and allow the students to select their own. In this manner, the teacher can individualize the work for his or her students. The important point in selecting a particular strategy is that it must be purposeful and meaningful to the lesson. Teachers must carefully plan the implementation steps that will work to improve student levels of achievement.

Creating effective strategies takes careful planning and consideration. Other research-based strategies should be considered, such as peer tutoring, guided notes, direct instruction, or computer-based instruction, to name a few. Guided notes, for instance, may best be utilized in a lecture-type class. Guided notes are outlines of textbook chapters or teacher lessons that leave spaces in the information where students supply the details. This practice has shown to increase student engagement. It has been shown that students who are actively engaged learn more than students who are passive.

This is the type of process that must be followed in creating effective strategy. Much time and effort must go into the planning phase to facilitate learning and to achieve the best possible results. The SPT or perhaps another group or committee should spend time researching the strategies that have proven to be effective. Along with this, providing the necessary professional development and monitoring the use of the strategies will ensure that the desired changes can be achieved.

Building Effective Action Plans

The unique feature of this strategic planning process is the fact that action plans are included. Without action plans, you cannot thoroughly implement a strategic plan or measure its success. Most strategic planning processes follow the same general steps; however, they fall short of the mark by not including the all-important action plans. The purpose of the action plan is to take the performance measure targets and translate them into action steps. The action steps will delineate exactly how the strategy will be implemented, the resources needed, who is responsible, how the step will be evaluated, and the timeline for carrying out or completing the strategy. When you have written plans, there is a greater likelihood that implementation will take place because it is known that what is measured or monitored is more likely to be carried out and ultimately, achieved. Utilizing action plans also indicates that you are proactively planning for student learning based on their needs. For these reasons, you need to ensure that the action plans are a part of the strategic process in order to achieve the greatest results. When strategies and action steps are clearly delineated, people are much more likely to understand their responsibilities, therefore, much more likely to implement the strategies and action steps according to the plan.

You may have been involved in a planning endeavor where a team or committee has written the plan but those implementing the plan were not involved. With this type of process, the plan is more likely to fail. If the teachers have not been a part of the development of the plan or the strategies, they will not feel as though they own the plan. Everyone who plays a part in implementing the plan must have a hand in the planning process in order to feel a sense of ownership. While all teachers may not be involved in the actual writing of the building plan, they should, nonetheless, contribute to the effort. There must be avenues for seeking and acquiring input from teachers prior to the action plans being written. When teachers and staff members are a part of the process, they will support the plan and feel a sense of responsibility for its success. Hold subject area meetings where teachers can provide input.

When writing the action plans, the SPT members should keep in mind that the math teachers, for instance, are not the only people who may work on the math goal. Other subject areas can easily incorporate math strategies into their content areas. Content areas, such as science or physical education, can play a part in the math strategies. Be sure to ask a lot of questions of the team and of the content area teachers to ensure all topics are explored. Ask pertinent questions, such as are there particular grade levels involved? What additional content areas can incorporate strategies related to this goal? Is the measure realistic and attainable for this subject area? The action plan is the place to clearly articulate the specifics of what will be done to achieve the goals. The strategies need to be inclusive of all facets of the organization that will be involved in achieving the goal, ranging from purchasing materials to after school study programs and everything in between.

There are actually two separate levels of action plans within the strategic plan: the building action and the classroom action plan. The SPT is responsible for creating the building level action plan and has been discussed above. Now it is time to focus on the classroom level action plan. With the building level action plan in hand, each classroom teacher will write his or her own classroom action plan. These plans will be based on the strategies delineated in the building plan and will include specific strategies to incorporate for individuals or groups of students. Content teachers should work together as they craft the action steps to ensure strategies will be implemented consistently. The classroom plans should be written to encompass a shorter period of time, such as a quarter, to enable teachers to tailor their plans to the changing needs of their students. Classroom action plans should be reviewed by the administration and SPT members.

Action Plan Format

To write detailed action steps, refer to the following information as a guide. Each action step should consist of the following:

1. Strategies: A brief statement for each of the strategies to be followed.
2. Implementation Steps: This section should detail (very specifically) the individual steps as to how the strategy will be accomplished. There can be more than one implementation step for each strategy.
3. Resources: What resources will be needed to ensure this step is accomplished in terms of financial or human resources?
4. Person(s) Responsible: Who is in charge of making certain this step is completed?
5. Evaluation / Indicator of Success: How will you know this step has been successfully completed?
6. Timeline / Date Completed / Status: When will this step be started and ended? (List dates for each of the steps or actions) limit the use of the word "ongoing."

To illustrate the process of completing the action plan, take a look at the example of improving achievement in eighth-grade math.

Example:

> Goal 1: The passage rate for the eighth-grade math students on the state assessment will improve by 10 percent each year of the three-year plan.

If you have multiple grade levels with which to work, you can state the goal for all grade levels to be the same or customize the standard for each grade level as appropriate.

Action Plan for Math Goal

Strategies	Implementation Steps	Resources Needed	Person(s) Responsible	Evaluation / Indicators of Success	Timeline
1.1 Teachers will differentiate instruction using flexible grouping, team teaching, cooperative learning, and independent work.	1.1a Math teachers will structure math classrooms to offer options for students based on their individual needs. 1.1b After pretesting, students will choose 3 activities from the list. Choice board, stations, independent activities, PowerPoint presentations, blogs, and portfolios will be offered to students based on their needs.	1.1a Materials for stations, computer programs at individual student level, manipulatives, and materials for group projects. 1.1b List of students and their pretest scores 1.1c Individualized activity list for each student	1.1a 8th grade teachers' (names) monitored by team leader.	1.1a Students will complete a set number of practice activities. 1.1b Students will complete each project-based activity with 90% accuracy.	1.1a Units 1, 2, and 3 in quarter 1. 1.1b Units 4, 5, and 6 in quarter 2. 1.1c Units 7, 8, and 9 in quarter 3. 1.1d Unit 10 in quarter 4.

1.2 Math teachers will pretest and posttest students at the beginning and end of each unit of study.	1.2a Students will engage in the unit pretests and posttests to determine growth.	1.2a Pretest and posttest materials	1.2a 8th grade math teachers' (names).	1.2a All students will earn a score of 90% or better on the unit posttests.	1.2a Pretest and posttest dates:
1.3 Teachers will make use of technology in the math classrooms.	1.3a Students will complete "Real Math" computer program activities based on need.	1.3a "Real Math" computer program. 1.3b Teacher assistant.	1.3a Teacher assistant will monitor and record progress	1.3a Students will record a 90% or better score on each of the program assessments.	1.3a Teachers will indicate timeline in classroom action plans.
1.4 Teachers will create an environment that supports high standards.	1.4a Teachers will vary the content with engaging activities.	1.4a Smart-boards, video, computers	1.4a Math teachers (names)	1.4a 95% of students will engage in and complete required activities for each unit. 1.4b Unit activity checklist	1.4a Units of study as indicated in 1.1a
1.5 Math teachers will engage in weekly team meetings.	1.5a Discuss various concepts each week to utilize in class: flexible grouping, differentiated instruction, team teaching.	1.5a Team meeting protocol. 1.5b Resources on each topic.	1.5a Math teachers (names) 1.5b Team leader will conduct meetings	1.5a Team meeting notes.	1.5a In full use by week 5 of 1st quarter then weekly through the year.

Figure 5.7. Building action plan example.

Once the building level action plans are completed, classroom teachers will work with their subject area teachers to create classroom action plans. While each teacher may have individual differences based on student needs, the strategies and action steps should be consistent across the content area.

8th Grade Math Classroom Action Plan

Teacher: _____

Strategies	Implemen-tation Steps	Resources Needed	Person(s) Responsible	Evaluation / Indicators of Success	Timeline
1. Differentiate instruction using flexible grouping, team teaching, cooperative learning, and independent work.	1.1a Provide a variety of instructional practices to enhance learning to include flexible grouping and assignments, projects, and presentations.	1.1a Computer programs at individual student level, manipulatives, group projects.	1.1a Math teacher	1.1a Classroom observations by admin. 1.1b Assignment checklist. 1.1c Participation in a variety of activities.	Quarter 1, unit 1, 2, and 3
1.2 Pretest and posttest students at the beginning and end of each unit of study.	1.2a Unit 1, 2, and 3 pretests. 1.2b Unit 1, 2, and 3 posttests.	1.2a Testing materials 1.2b Answer keys	1.2a Math teacher and instructional assistant.	1.2a 90% or higher on posttests for each unit.	1.2a Dates for Pretests and posttests.
1.3 Use technology in the math classrooms.	1.3a Based on results of unit pretests, students will be assigned specific computer programs two times per week	1.3a Posttest results. 1.3b Computers 1.3c Computer programs	1.3a Math teacher 1.3b Instructional assistant	1.3a Scores on computer program activities. 1.3b Posttest results. 1.3c Student use of technology during observations.	1.3a Dates for units 1, 2, and 3 in quarter 1.

1.4 Create an environment that supports high standards.	1.4a Communicate clear learning goals. 1.4b Link learning activities to the goals. 1.4c Vary the activities to engage students.	1.4a Materials related to current unit of study.	1.4 Math teacher	1.4a Use of instructional time. 1.4b Students can articulate learning goals.	1.4a Daily
1.5 Engage in weekly team meetings.	1.5 Teacher attends weekly team meeting each Tuesday during 3rd period.	1.5a Team meeting protocol 1.5b Unit of study resources to collaborate with other teachers.	1.5a Math teachers	1.5a Team meeting notes 1.5b Evidence of collaboration in lesson plans.	1.5a Weekly monitoring of lesson plans 1.5b Quarterly monitoring of action plans.

Figure 5.8. Classroom action plan example.

The first draft of your plan will most likely not be your final draft. Once you have completed a draft of the plan, share it with your staff and ask for reactions, suggestions, and ideas for improvements. Create a process for how you will seek the feedback in order to facilitate the gathering of information in a timely manner. As staff members have suggestions, they should place the information in writing with specific details on their ideas.

Many times, teachers are too busy to take the time to review the information; therefore, another approach to gathering feedback is to plan time during a staff meeting that will allow teachers to meet together and discuss the elements of the plan. The benefit of such a meeting is twofold. First, you can ensure that the plan will be reviewed. Second, a dialogue with colleagues can bring about ideas that may not be generated if teachers were to carry out this activity alone.

Provide a window of opportunity for feedback that is long enough to incorporate a staff meeting, or additional staff meetings, if necessary, yet brief enough to keep the process moving along. If suggestions are made that cannot be used at the current time, continue to collect the information on the parking lot list and maintain the list of ideas for future reference.

Professional development and training is another issue that must be addressed. If a strategy, for instance, is to implement a new computer program for math, there is much to do to prepare. Teachers will need to be instructed on the use of the program through training and professional development sessions. The implementation of the new program should be built into the action plan as one of the strategies under the math goal. Time must be allocated for teachers to learn and feel comfortable with the new program.

Communicating the Action Plans

You have spent the last several months creating an outstanding plan that will bring about great improvements and results over the next several years. Now, you have just one more important step you must be sure to take before the implementation of the plan begins. You must communicate the strategic plan with the school community in preparation for implementation.

Along with the SPT, determine the best way to communicate the plan with everyone in the organization. A meeting involving the entire staff is strongly recommend where everyone hears the details of the plan from you, the instructional leader, and the SPT, officially for the first time. Distribute copies to everyone and review the full document. You may want to assign certain sections to members of the SPT to explain. To enhance the presentation of the strategic plan, you could create a video, a PowerPoint presentation, or a Prezi presentation to accompany the handouts and present the plan with interest and enthusiasm. Subsequently, consider small group meetings, such as team or department meetings, to clarify responsibilities, answer questions, and dispel any fears and anxieties that may exist. People may not want to ask questions in a whole group setting but in a smaller, more familiar setting, such as a team meeting, questions and concerns can be addressed and clarified. If you are beginning the implementation of the plan at the start of a new school year, arrange a special event to introduce it. Consider the scheduling of this event to allow sufficient time for everyone to prepare for the changes ahead. A good time to hold the event is near the end of the current school year. While many people are anxiously anticipating summer break, you can begin to generate excitement for the upcoming school year if properly handled. Talk up the plan with the students, too, and let them know to expect some exciting changes in the new school year.

Celebrate the completion of the written plan as this is a huge milestone in the process. Praise the staff for their hard work and efforts in the past, and present the plan as a way of focusing efforts to achieve desired results in the coming years. Reassure everyone that this is the instrument that will guide the work throughout the school over the next several years. Undoubtedly, work will need to be done during the summer months in preparation for the start of the plan at the beginning of the school year. If at all possible, set aside extra funds to be able to provide a stipend to the SPT or other members of the staff who are able to do specific work over the summer to ensure you are ready for implementation the first day of school. Within your action plans, specifically detail the work to be done prior to the start of the school year. With that said, you may technically begin the strategic plan in June or once the current school year has ended rather than the start of the new school year because some of the strategies and action steps will need to be completed prior to the beginning of the school year. For example, if you are purchasing a new resource or hiring new teachers, these steps must be completed before the start of the school year.

Chapter Summary

The written plan will be the guide by which all work is done. Although you will have an SPT to conduct the actual writing of the building plan, input is necessary to gather from everyone who will be responsible for the implementation. For example, a math goal will require that discussions take place with the math teachers to identify strategies that have worked in the past that should be included in the plan as well as new strategies that have been researched. Other subject areas should be identified to assist with the goals. For example, science teachers can incorporate strategies to assist in reaching math goals and these should be written into the plan. The SPT should be divided into three goals groups for the writing of the plan. Concentrating on one area will permit the SPT members to become more familiar with one particular area and it will divide the responsibility among the SPT.

This chapter details the process of completing the strategic plan including the building level and classroom level action plans. The building action plan portion of the strategic plan serves as the daily guide for the work that is to be accomplished. It will contain strategies for each goal and specific action steps for each strategy. Teachers and staff members must know their individual responsibilities related to the strategies. Each teacher will base his or her classroom action plan on the information from the building plan. Content area teachers should work together to create classroom action plan strategies and action steps to ensure fidelity of implementation.

The final written plan should be thoroughly communicated with the school community in preparation for implementation.

CHAPTER 6

Implementing the Plan

There are a number of resources on the topic of writing a strategic plan. You can find out how to create a mission statement and how to write your goals, but when it comes down to putting your plan into action, resources become very limited on the subject. In this chapter, you will find ways to accomplish the most important step in the plan: implementation.

At last you are ready to begin the implementation phase of the strategic plan. The plan that took a great deal of time and effort to prepare should be considered your roadmap for improving student achievement as well as accomplishing the additional goals you have set out to attain in your building. The strategic plan must be the guide by which all work is performed. Each individual strategy has been broken down into manageable action steps, each step has been delegated to specific people, and each person knows his or her role and responsibility. Too often an enormous amount of time and resources are spent in the process of planning only to find that the document ends up on a shelf with past programs that were attempted or is otherwise not being utilized as it should.

The previous chapters discussed communicating the plan, but a few words are necessary here to restate the importance of communication. Communication of the plan is not something to do one time and assume that everyone knows exactly what to do. As important as it was during the planning phase of this process, communication during the implementation becomes even more important. It must be an ongoing part of the plan all throughout the implementation. Once all the staff members have initially been presented with the strategic plan, they will then be prepared to create their individual classroom plans. Once these are completed and reviewed, they will be ready to begin proactively implementing the plan. Make the plan as public as possible and call attention to it often. Again, if you are initiating the plan at the beginning of a new school year, you will need to make all conversations and meetings center on the plan. Many teachers start working in the summer prior to their official start date to prepare their classrooms for the upcoming school year. As individual teachers come in, take the time to hold conversations with them regarding their particular role in the strategic process. Discuss their thoughts and concerns regarding the implementation of the strategic plan and to discuss their individual classroom action plans. One-on-one conversations can be extremely beneficial to you as you assess staff members' knowledge of the plan and their comfort level in beginning the implementation.

To be effective, the plan must remain fresh in the minds of all those involved in its implementation, which essentially is everyone in the organization. The strategic plan must be looked at and talked about every day. All members of the organization need to know that the plan is important and that the plan is essential to student achievement and school improvement. Create ways each and every day to engage in discussions with teachers, students, parents, and staff and create engaging opportunities among the staff for discussion and collaboration. The plan must be pervasive throughout the school community. As the plan progresses throughout the year, there will be a need for additional training or professional development. For example, as new strategies come into play, make certain that everyone responsible for their implementation is ready and able to carry them out. Do not leave this to chance. Stay on top of the plan so that when new strategies are to go into effect, everyone will be ready. You may want to have a person, possibly a member of the SPT or another administrator, responsible for the timeline who will keep you apprised of the new strategies in plenty of time to be prepared.

In the process of creating the plan, you did all that was possible to get everyone on board and geared up for the changes that are to occur during the implementation. Some people may have criticized the plan as extra work or saw it as a phase that would come and go. Not so with your strategic plan. It is not a phase, a fad, or the next best program to try, but will be a way of life and a way of doing business in your school. A strategic plan is not a program but is a process for implementing programs or procedures. It is the manner in which the work will be accomplished. This is a great opportunity to emphasize the phrase "work smarter, not harder." You have no doubt seen people who stay late every day but don't seem to make any headway. The results they achieve are not in direct correlation to how long or how hard they work. Refer back to the time management activity in chapter 1 as a way to motivate staff to work more efficiently. Be very sure that you have communicated along the way the fact that the strategic planning goals, strategies, and actions are not an addition to the work that is currently being done, but the goals, strategies, and actions will replace current practices. Those implementing the plan should understand that the plan is not a new layer of work on top of what is already in place but that the plan serves as a different, and confidently, better way to accomplish the goals.

In your initial staff meeting for the year, set out your expectations clearly and precisely then enthusiastically review the plan. Include SPT members in the presentation. It is well known that teachers respond well to other teachers presenting information rather than receiving the information only from the administration. Teacher-to-teacher presentations are typically well-received by colleagues because generally there is a greater degree of trust among teacher-to-teacher interactions as opposed to management-teacher interactions. This is particularly true if you are a fairly new administrator in your building or if you have a particularly strong and active union. In addition, displaying unity between the administration and teachers who serve on the SPT will go a long way in building the trust that is much needed in this process.

You, along with the SPT, need to convey through conversations and demonstrate through actions that the initiatives that have been established in the plan are essential to success. Use the creativity of your team to find ways to inspire and motivate the staff to embrace the plan and get involved 100 percent. Create signs or posters that can be placed in classrooms and other areas of the building that will serve as reminders to everyone of the work that is necessary to reach the goals. Post, for example, the mission statement in every classroom and post the goals in common areas of the building. Each staff member should have a copy of his or her own responsibilities derived from the action steps as well as a copy of his or her own classroom action plans that have been reviewed by the SPT and the administration. Craft strategies that will demonstrate to the students that the plan is a priority. New actions and processes will be taking the place of old ones. Just as you worked to secure teacher buy-in and commitment, you must do the same with students as well. For both of these reasons, the beginning of the school year is the optimal time to initiate the strategic plan. As a word of caution, nevertheless, be certain that your entire school community is prepared for the launch of the plan so that it is not a surprise to anyone.

As the principal, you cannot be all places at all times. You need to entrust staff members to positions of responsibility and oversight in order to successfully monitor the strategies. A chain of command should be followed which has already been spelled out within the planning document. These key people will monitor the processes and keep you updated on their observations. This must be handled clearly and cautiously so as to prevent friction from developing between staff members. The chain of command roles must be clearly delineated; otherwise, the leaders could be viewed negatively among the staff. Most people hold the belief, and rightly so, that teachers enter the business to help kids. For the vast majority, this is true. Nonetheless, an atmosphere of competitiveness can occur if collaboration and cooperation are not present.

Looking back to the topic of preparing the staff, here are a few key points to remember.

- Communicate frequently and regularly.
- Post visual reminders related to the strategic plan, such as the mission and goals, throughout the building.
- Create a chain of command which delineates the person(s) responsible for monitoring the strategies being implemented.
- Review monthly or quarterly classroom action plans.

➤ Frequently engage in conversation about the action plans with those responsible for their implementation.

➤ Demonstrate through your actions that the plan is a priority.

The Administration and the Strategic Plan

The administrative team in your building plays a huge role in the successful implementation of the strategic plan. There is nothing more important to your administration than the improvement of student achievement. Whether it is you alone, or a team of several administrators, set your expectations and insist that priority be placed on the implementation of all facets of the plan. Administrators must be involved in the monitoring of instruction on a daily basis; consequently, make certain the administrative team has a thorough understanding of all of the action steps within the plan and that each administrator knows what to observe. Administrators should also assist with the review of the classroom action plans. Divide the review and monitoring responsibilities among the administrative staff by assigning administrators to specific subject areas or grade levels, for example.

The administration is responsible for identifying those who may not be implementing the plan appropriately or according to the plan. When deficiencies are discovered, steps must be taken to correct the matter as quickly as possible. Typically, deficiencies occur because a teacher lacks the skills or knowledge necessary for optimal performance. Strategies need to be available to assist teachers that will bridge the gap in knowledge or skill. Examples of strategies to consider are modeling, mentoring, team teaching, professional development, workshops, seminars, or coursework. At times, the deficiency may be due to a teacher's lack of interest or a lack of belief in his ability to make a difference for students. In a case such as this, serious conversation needs to occur with the teacher to uncover and remediate the exact issue. The administration should support teachers in making the improvements needed to carry out the strategic plan for the benefit of the students and of the school's success.

The Teachers/Staff and the Strategic Plan

Teachers and staff members are on the front line every day. Likewise, they will be the front line of the strategic plan implementation. It is imperative that they are not only knowledgeable about the plan but are also comfortable with managing the implementation of the specific action steps pertaining to their particular job or role. In addition, each teacher is responsible for developing and implementing his or her own classroom action plans. Teachers should involve students in reaching the goals of the plan by engaging them in goal setting in both academic and personal areas.

The teachers' responsibility is to implement all steps in the action plans to the letter. They should openly and honestly reflect on their capabilities and identify any weaknesses in terms of their ability to implement the plan. As difficult as this can be, the school must possess a climate where trust is present in order to help teachers feel comfortable with identifying their areas of weakness and seeking assistance to improve. The motivation for identifying a teacher's weaknesses has to be a focus on the improvement of instruction rather than on evaluation of the teacher. Resources as noted above should be made available to teachers that will address their needs. Teachers must be willing to take advantage of any assistance available to help them improve. As delicate as these situations can be, everyone must be willing to improve or help others improve without fear of weaknesses being held against them. Involve teachers in planning motivational activities and incentives for implementing strategies and reaching goals.

The Students and the Strategic Plan

Students will play an important role in the implementation of your strategic plan. Work with the student leadership in the building, if such organizations exist, to assist you in promoting and carrying out the strategic plan. At the beginning of the school year, you should hold meetings with students to clearly outline the plans that will impact their education and their daily routines. Do not assume that students know how you want them to behave or what you expect them to do. For example, if one of your goals is to improve the orderliness of class changes during the school day, teach the students what you expect them to do when moving from one class to the next or teach them specific procedures to follow when going to the cafeteria for lunch. Students should be engaged in academic and personal goal setting in each class. Involve students in planning motivational activities or perhaps incentives for students who reach certain goals.

The School Community and the Strategic Plan

The school community, consisting of parents, business partners, local businesses, and community leaders, to name a few, should be well aware of the strategic plan. In terms of assistance, the best thing the school community can do is support the plan. Support can take many forms. From parents, you want support to include talking with teachers, ensuring their students' homework is complete, or sending students to school ready to learn. Support from business and community could come in the form of financial or human resources. Many businesses lend support to schools where a partnership will benefit both the school and the business. Make your needs known to the school community and identify specific ways in which community members or organizations can be helpful.

Keys to Successful Implementation

How can you be sure that the strategic plan you and your team worked so hard to create will be implemented? There are essential elements to which attention must be paid. Be sure to institute the following suggestions to ensure successful implementation.

➤ Leadership: Who is responsible for the plan? Leadership can and should come from a variety of places within the organization. Obviously, the administration serves as one level of leadership, but beyond that there are other types of leaders within the organization. The appointed leaders, for example, department heads or team leaders, can assist in monitoring strategy implementation within their own departments or teams. Teachers who possess expertise or experience in specific areas can serve as an informal leader to other members of the staff. Most often, these teachers are willing and eager to extend themselves to others who may need assistance. They may be able to model certain strategies or work with a partner in a team teaching role with someone who can learn from their work. Leaders, whether formal or informal, can assist the staff in many ways. Leaders can

- assist other teachers with writing classroom action plans,
- observe strategies as they are implemented,
- coach those who need assistance with knowledge or skills,
- motivate staff who need extra encouragement,
- monitor outcomes and progress,
- support others to build confidence, and
- challenge those who are struggling.

Leadership from others in the organization is needed, as well, in order to make certain the plan is followed. Administrators cannot be solely responsible for monitoring the plan.

➢ Commitment, ownership, and accountability: Place the responsibility for success on everyone. This process is a total team effort that must be diligently followed and carried out. A feeling of ownership will generate a feeling of commitment. When people feel that they are a part of or "own" something, they are much more likely to embrace it and take care to see it through. Everyone needs to feel a sense of ownership of the strategic plan, but beyond that, everyone needs to feel they have a stake in the success of the plan. By holding everyone accountable, you are showing them that the work is important, and they will feel a sense of responsibility.

➤ Belief in the plan: When properly presented and communicated, you can create interest and support and, therefore, belief in the plan. If you, members of the SPT, or other leaders have presented the plan enthusiastically with strong convictions, these attitudes and beliefs will be accepted more readily by the rest of the staff and community. If, on the other hand, you create a written plan, distribute the plan, then expect it to work, you will fall short of your goals due to the mere fact that there are not strong convictions or beliefs in the plan. This relates back to the Pygmalion effect and the attribution theory presented earlier in this book. Expectations are everything and can be the difference between success and failure.

➤ Communication: Communication encompasses a number of matters in and around the strategic planning process. Not only is communication important prior to beginning the implementation of the plan but it is also important throughout the implementation. Staff members need to communicate what seems to be working, what is not working, what problems arise, possible solutions to problems, the need for assistance, the positive results that are gained, and so on. Find new ways to discuss the plan, recognize teachers and students for improvements, and hold contests or challenges to keep the plan interesting.

Communication can occur through:

- Daily announcements: Reminders to students and staff, achievements, accomplishments, or progress made.
- Newsletters: Reports to parents and community regarding needs of the school or the progress achieved.
- Staff meetings: Set aside time where teachers can share their successes with others.
- Staff bulletins: Inspirational thoughts to teachers that motivate and encourage them to continue to work the plan, progress being made,

or special recognition of staff members generating exceptional results.

- Website: post news and updates regularly on the school website.

➤ Monitoring progress along the way: Build in regular checkpoints, for example, monthly or quarterly meetings where you will review progress by analyzing available data. Monthly or quarterly checks will determine whether or not you are on track to meet your goals. The monthly or quarterly classroom action plans should be submitted, reviewed, and discussed with teachers. If you find that some are straying from the plan, you can quickly identify and resolve the issues and get everyone back on track. Close monitoring lets everyone know that the plan is important and there is an expectation that full implementation is needed. Frequent monitoring will keep the process firmly on track. Hold regularly scheduled meetings with the SPT to discuss and monitor the process and the progress.

➤ Praise and recognition: Praise and recognition are critical elements for increasing productivity. Everyone has the need to be recognized and with recognition comes a feeling of accomplishment. Praise and recognition should be given to staff members based on performance and results and should be done on a regular basis.

➤ Patience: While a sense of urgency must be present, do not expect to implement all of the strategies at one time and do not expect everyone to implement the strategies perfectly; otherwise, you will experience much frustration. You must find the balance between patience and urgency. Initiate the strategies over time so that each strategy can be fully implemented. It is much better to implement a few strategies and do them well, rather than try to implement too many of them at one time and the process fails. During your monthly or quarterly checkpoints, be sure to discuss the implementation and whether or not new strategies are ready to be implemented. You can and should adjust the timeline when necessary.

Why Strategic Plans Fail

With the time and effort expended in creating and implementing your strategic plan, the last thing you want to happen is to see the plan fail. The possibility of failure will be extremely small when the elements discussed above are in place. There are, nonetheless, several areas to watch to prevent failure of the strategic plan from happening in your school. If the plan fails, you will not be able to reach the goals you set out to achieve. Strategic plans may fail due to:

➤ Lack of Input: Input from all constituencies must be sought when creating the plan. If people feel they have not been included or feel that they have not had a say, they will be less likely to support or implement the plan and the plan could fail.

➤ Lack of Definition: Lack of clearly defined goals and lack of clearly defined steps to carry out the goals can cause the plan to fail.

➤ Lack of Clarity: If people do not know the expectations in terms of the gains that need to be made, the goals are less likely to be met. When roles and expectations are not clearly delineated, confusion and frustration can result, and the plan will not be implemented as intended.

➤ Lack of Communication: Failure to properly communicate is the most common mistake that will keep the plan from working. Communication was a topic in virtually all phases of the strategic planning process. A lack of communication in any phase of the process will be detrimental.

➤ Lack of Detail: When people do not know their exact responsibilities, you will find that there will not be full implementation of the plan. When responsibilities are not specific enough, people will not be able to follow through completely.

➤ Lack of Interest: As time goes on, interest can wane if the plan is not bolstered. When the plan is not communicated or discussed regularly, staff members may think the plan is no longer important.

➤ Lack of Monitoring: If monitoring practices are not in place or are not carried out regularly, staff members may get the idea that the plan is no longer important. If monitoring slows down, implementation likewise will slow down.

Chapter Summary

As important as it is to have an excellently written plan, it is even more important to ensure that the strategic plan progresses to the implementation stage. Oftentimes, schools will celebrate the completion of the written document and see this as an end. On the contrary, this is just the beginning of the real work at hand.

As an administrator, you must set expectations for the implementation of the plan. You should be familiar with all aspects of the plan because you will be responsible for monitoring the daily activities as you visit classrooms and observe teaching and learning. Teachers and staff members need to possess a good understanding of the goals and strategies and be able to implement each and every action step in his or her specific area. Staff members should seek assistance if they are unsure about their responsibilities or if they need help with implementing the plan. Students also play an important role in the strategic plan. Student leadership can assist with planning motivational activities or incentives for students.

Keys to successful implementation are leadership; commitment, ownership, and accountability; belief in the plan; communication; monitoring progress; praise and recognition; and patience. To avoid failure be sure to gather input from all staff, clearly define roles and responsibilities, communicate the expectations, find new ways to motivate teachers and staff members, maintain interest in the process, and continue to monitor the process and the progress.

CHAPTER 7

Monitoring and Evaluating the Plan

Monitoring and evaluation practices need to be built into your strategic plan. While there is no single best way to monitor and evaluate your plan, the exact process you establish for your particular setting will be determined by you and the SPT. You will be able to select from a variety of options to find what will work best for your school. While suggested options are examples of various methods and possibilities, all of the methods do not need to be employed nor should you feel obligated to implement them exactly as detailed. With a good understanding of what it means to monitor and evaluate your plan, you can best decide when to perform them and how you will go about accomplishing them. Even though monitoring and evaluation seem to go together hand in hand, they are essentially two separate elements that have their own purpose within the strategic planning process. The two, nevertheless, are oftentimes used in tandem to inform an organization how it is doing in reference to the strategies and action plans that are implemented and to report the results that are achieved. The fundamental elements in monitoring and evaluating your plan are to know

- ➤ what you want to implement
- ➤ what you want to measure
- ➤ what you want to achieve
- ➤ how you want to achieve it
- ➤ whether or not it was achieved

In terms of this strategic planning process, monitoring is used to ensure the plan is implemented as intended and to gather information needed to make judgments about the progress. Evaluating uses the information that has been gathered through the monitoring activities to measure progress and to investigate how the process has worked. With that being said, remember that there are multiple means of both monitoring and evaluating depending on your particular situation and needs. From simplistic to complex procedures, make the monitoring and evaluating processes work for you. It is not necessary to do a full-scale evaluation each year or even at the end of the three year period of the plan if your monitoring practices are providing the information you need.

Monitoring can be viewed as a formative and ongoing process, which takes place throughout the course of the plan. Evaluating is associated with a summative and formal process and is generally conducted at the end of the plan or at the end of each year. Each will be discussed separately, but here are a few of the major differences between the two.

Monitoring	Evaluating
Performed during implementation	Reviews progress and outcomes
Ongoing data collection and review	Examines long-term results
Ensures proper implementation	Reveals how the plan was/was not successful
Informs decisions during the process	Reveals why the plan was/was not successful
Undertaken more frequently than evaluation	Examines how the process worked

Figure 7.1. Differences between monitoring and evaluating.

Monitoring

It is said that what is measured or monitored is what is accomplished. The planning document and action plans you and your team created included provisions for measuring progress on each of the strategies and action steps. To get the most from your strategic plan, you must be certain that the provisions were written concisely, utilizing appropriate metrics. You will find that the SMART goals you wrote into your plan earlier in the process will be valuable in this stage because you will know exactly what you wanted to achieve and how you wanted to go about achieving it.

Monitoring should take place regularly throughout the implementation. There are two purposes for monitoring:

➤ monitoring the implementation of the plan and
➤ monitoring student progress.

Each of these purposes is important for a number of reasons. Where monitoring the implementation of the plan is concerned, frequent checks will let you know if the strategies are being implemented as specified in the plan. If the evidence shows that the strategies are being implemented as intended, you can later determine if they are achieving the desired results. When monitoring reveals that strategies are not being implemented according to plan, you will know that it is time to intervene.

Monitoring will provide critical evidence of the impact that the strategies employed have had toward meeting your goals. The monitoring process can pinpoint where deficiencies may exist in student progress. For example, having eight teachers teaching math at the same grade level can produce a wide range of results, particularly if some teachers are employing a variety of teaching strategies and are not consistently implementing the strategies as indicated in the building plan. During the implementation of your strategic plan, the eight teachers were to employ a specific strategy that was intended to improve student answers on constructed response questions. Through the monitoring of the results, you found that four teachers produced high results, two teachers produced average results, and two teachers produced low results on a student assessment at the end of the first quarter. Furthermore, through classroom observations, you discovered that the two teachers who produced low results had difficulty following and implementing a number of the action steps in their classrooms. From this information, you can further investigate to identify what worked in the classrooms that yielded higher results and whether or not those teachers implemented the strategies as designed in the plan. This example is quite simplistic as you may not be able to detect the problems quite so easily. However, this example illustrates the point that your teachers must know what they are expected to do and you must be able to establish that they are following the plan when you conduct the monitoring activities. Regular monitoring provides the information you need during the process so that adjustments can be made, if necessary. Instead of waiting until the end of the year or the end of the three-year plan to find out how well the students performed, you will have the evidence needed to indicate exactly where they stand during the implementation. The results you do or do not achieve will be clear to see through the monitoring activities you apply.

The above example also brings into question the timing of the data to be gathered. If one or more of your academic goals has been based on a state assessment that is administered once a year, you cannot wait until the next administration of the state assessment to compare results and determine whether or not your students are making progress. As discussed in chapter 4, the use of one or more of the variety of tiered assessments, such as a district assessment, should be administered at least quarterly to provide data for monitoring purposes. Assessments can be short, teacher-created tests that cover the standards taught during the quarter or you may purchase premade assessments that are aligned to the standards you teach. Pretests at the beginning and posttests at the end of each unit of study can provide data to identify the need for further intervention. In any case, the questions should mirror those given on the state assessments in order to ensure that comparable data are reviewed.

Gathering current data through the monitoring process will inform your decision making. In other words, if the data show gains have been achieved and the strategies have been implemented as designed in the plan, you will know your strategies have been effective. If results are varied, you will know that further investigation is needed to discover why the variances exist. You may need to make the decision to revise one or several of your strategies if the intended results are not evident. Again, do not rush to make changes immediately, particularly if you are very early in the process. These are not easy decisions, but before making changes, a useful strategy to apply in this situation is to conference with the teachers. Referring to the example above, meet individually with each of the eight math teachers to discuss classroom action plans and results from their own classes. A group discussion could also be useful. Ask the teachers about the implementation of the strategies and what they view as their successes and their challenges regarding student results. Caution must be taken with the information you gather regarding individual teachers and individual students. Any personal information should be handled in a professional manner. You need to be certain that trust and respect are maintained for others in the process.

The monitoring process can inspire ongoing improvement. When the data show improvements, staff will be encouraged and will realize that their efforts are indeed effectual. Momentum can be built on the documented progress, which will encourage further execution of the plan. Watch, though, that complacency does not set in when positive results are achieved early on. If results are positive, teachers may get the idea that their work is done, nevertheless their efforts must continue in order to sustain the improvements. Be sure to communicate this to the staff.

Monitoring the strategic plan should occur all throughout the implementation of the plan and should be carried out by a variety of people. As noted, the principal and administration should conduct monitoring procedures as part of their daily routine. As the principal, when you move throughout the building each day, you can check in on a number of classrooms, even if only for a few minutes each. By regularly checking in on classes, teachers and students will know that the process is important and that monitoring of teaching and learning are taking place. The information you gather through these classroom visits and other monitoring activities will provide the evidence you need as you assess how the strategies are implemented.

The following illustrates the benefits of monitoring the strategic plan.

Benefits of Monitoring the Strategic Plan

- Informs your decision making
- Conveys the importance of the plan
- Inspires continued improvement
- Ensures results are being met
- Enables adjustments to be made along the way
- Provides critical information for the evaluation process

The Process for Monitoring the Plan

As the building leader, you must be familiar with all facets of the action plans because, ultimately, you are held responsible for the outcomes in your school. Although you will have designated staff responsible for each strategy within the action plan, you should formally and informally monitor the implementation of the strategies on a regular basis to ensure that the plan is being followed as specified. Administrative monitoring can be accomplished through classroom observations, walkthroughs, and conferences with teachers and staff members. Be sure you are familiar with the strategies that are to be implemented, and after visiting a classroom, whether formally or informally, be certain to hold at least a brief discussion with the teacher to talk about positive aspects and areas for improvement based on your observations. You may not be able to observe specific strategies each time you go into a classroom, yet teachers need to be able to articulate how they are utilizing the strategies. If not observed, set a time to return to see the strategies in action.

Teachers generally want to know how they are doing and where they stand. Communication is still extremely important as you monitor the implementation of the action plans. Provide feedback as immediately as possible following an observation, especially if there are concerns regarding the implementation. With your communication, speak candidly to those you observe not following the action plans as specified. In cases such as these, a more in-depth discussion and perhaps an implementation plan or improvement plan, which is a way to express your concerns in writing, for the teacher may be in order. On the other hand, teachers who are implementing the strategies as designed must be given feedback and encouragement to continue. Monitoring is a commitment to accountability for everyone in the school. By making yourself visible through conducting observation and communicating with feedback every day, your staff will understand the urgency of following through on each and every strategy.

Set a schedule for follow-up meetings and checkpoints that will take place during the implementation phase of the plan. You or the lead person of the SPT should communicate the meeting schedule with the team and reiterate exactly what they will be expected to provide. Communication is vitally important to maintain not only from the top down but also from bottom up. In other words, members of the SPT will need to gather data, feedback, and anecdotal information from those implementing the plan to bring to the monitoring meetings. Anecdotal records should be maintained with both positive accounts and areas of concern. In addition to discussions with staff members, a survey could be distributed that contains a set of questions on which all staff can respond, including a place for comments. Feedback of this nature can serve the school well in monitoring progress from a qualitative perspective. A sample survey is included in the workbook.

A good strategic plan alone does not ensure results, which speaks to the importance of the monitoring phase. Moreover, it must be understood that monitoring, in and of itself, will not ensure results either. Constant feedback and communication along with the monitoring activities will serve to keep the work on track. Be sure to follow through with the planned strategies for monitoring progress so as to support complete implementation of all strategies and action steps. Figure 7.3 will help to summarize the important points of monitoring your strategic plan.

Tips for Monitoring the Strategic Plan

- Be familiar with all aspects of the plan
- Visit classrooms frequently and regularly
- Discuss observations following each class visit
- Hold regularly scheduled follow-up SPT meetings and checkpoints
- Seek feedback from those implementing the plan
- Communicate, communicate, communicate

Evaluating

There is an ever-increasing demand for demonstrating improvements in test results as a measure of a school's effectiveness. In addition to monitoring, evaluating is another tool to assist you in illustrating your results along with determining how well your plan is working. It is not necessary for staff members to completely understand highly complex data analysis processes in order to make good decisions or judgments about the plan; however, a basic understanding such as that presented in chapter 4 will suffice. Evaluating, similar to monitoring, encompasses two specific areas:

> ➢ evaluation of the implementation of the plan and
> ➢ evaluation of the results achieved.

Evaluating the implementation of the plan can be a difficult task because in the school setting, strategic plans continue on from year to year. There is typically no end point as there may be with some programs, especially in business. However, an evaluation could be conducted after the three year period.

When it comes to evaluating of the results achieved, an important question to consider is *can the evaluation be done in a timely manner so as to be useful?* Oftentimes, the information needed to conduct the evaluation arrives too late to be of value in terms of revising or modifying the current strategic plan for the next school year. If you are waiting for state assessment results before making adjustments to the plan, you should continue the implementation of the plan as scheduled. Once the information is in hand, you can conduct your evaluation and make any modifications that are necessary, perhaps at the first quarterly review.

If you are able to gather the data needed for an evaluation at the end of the school year, the evaluation will support your accountability measures. This is essentially the comparison of what you planned to do against what actually has taken place, including how you accomplished what you did. It compares the actual results achieved to the goals that were set. You want to determine if you reached the goals you set out to accomplish. By simply looking at goals versus results, you will discover if, in fact, the goals were reached. Beyond that, however, if the goals were not reached, you will be able to find out where and why they were not by looking further into the results of individual standards and for individual students. This is easier said than done if accountability measures are not built into the plan. Therefore, to ensure accountability measures are in place, each person in the organization that plays a role in the strategic plan is named in the plan under the specific strategies for which he or she is responsible, as illustrated in chapter 5. While this may be intimidating to some, it is necessary to know who is responsible for each of the strategies so that intervention and assistance can be provided when the evaluation reveals weaknesses. In addition, student results for each teacher need to be made available for evaluation of individual student progress. From there, teachers will use these data to create their individual action plans for the next month or quarter.

Evaluation can be formative or summative. Formative evaluation occurs when an organization needs to check progress during the implementation of a plan. Summative evaluation occurs when an organization needs to assess results at the end of the implementation of a plan. In some cases, both formative and summative evaluations are utilized in the strategic planning process because information about what is happening during the plan as well as at the end of the plan may be necessary. A summative evaluation, however, tends to be associated with a formal program evaluation, which is conducted at the conclusion of a program. The model detailed in this book is well suited for involving mainly the formative type of evaluation. This is true because of the continuous nature of the strategic planning process which progresses from year to year without a true endpoint.

Another consideration for evaluation relates to who will be conducting the evaluation. The evaluation can be conducted internally or externally. An internal evaluation is conducted by people within the organization, most likely administrators, SPT, or specific evaluation personnel, if such exists within your district. An external evaluation is conducted by people outside the organization, perhaps by an outside consultant. In the majority of cases, a strategic plan is evaluated internally. External evaluations are typically conducted when a more formal or full program evaluation is needed at the end of a specific program.

Evaluating results can, at times, reveal unintended outcomes. Consider this example. The fifth-grade students, after a period of math instruction following the strategies set out in the action plans, were given an assessment. Once the assessments were scored, the teachers analyzed the data. One of the goals in the math area was to decrease the achievement gap between boys and girls. On this particular assessment, after reviewing the data, they found that the overall results for the girls increased and overall results for the boys remained essentially the same; therefore, the achievement gap actually increased rather than decreased. While everyone can celebrate the increase in achievement by the girls, they need to determine what happened with results of the boys. At this point, a review of not only the strategies but also a review of the teachers' implementation of the strategies must take place. Individual student's scores for each teacher's class should be analyzed: first by utilizing the frequency distribution analysis of the whole class, and second by using an item analysis for each student's responses, both of which were presented in chapter 4. The following figure displays some of the benefits you can expect by using evaluation practices.

Benefits of Evaluating the Strategic Plan

- Determines whether or not the strategies were successful
- Identifies whether or not the goals were appropriate
- Documents results
- Provides comparison data
- Presents a true picture of the school
- Delivers accountability

The Process for Evaluating the Plan

In terms of evaluation for this strategic planning model, both a formative approach and a summative approach could be used. Considering a three-year plan, a formative approach can be utilized at set times throughout each school year such as quarterly evaluations, and at the end of the first and second year. A summative approach could be utilized at the end of the first and second year or when you come to the end of the three-year plan. You and the SPT will need to determine the best option for the evaluation measures most suited for your own situation. You may decide to rely totally on a formative evaluation process since your strategic plan will continue on from year to year. Therefore, you can elect to utilize one of these options to approach the evaluation process.

Evaluation options:

1. Formative evaluation at the end of each quarter, summative evaluation at the end of each year.
2. Formative evaluation at the end of each quarter and at the end of the first and second years, summative evaluation at the end of the third year.
3. Formative evaluation at the end of each quarter and at the end of each year.

The first option should be used when you want a more formal appraisal of the results at the end of each school year. With this option, you could make changes to the action plans based on the summative results. At the end of each year of implementation, a summative approach may be employed to obtain an overall answer to the question of how effective the strategic plan has been over the period of one year. If a summative evaluation is conducted at the end of each year, results can be compared from one year to the next. The drawback, however, is that generally speaking, state assessment results are not available soon enough for the evaluation to take place at the end of the year and then prepare the necessary changes for the beginning of the next school year. You may, however, make use of school or district assessments that are conducted at the end of each unit or quarter.

The second option should be used when you want to declare an actual end of the three-year project. In this case, you should conduct the formative evaluation processes at the end of each quarter. This would indicate that you intend to run the strategic plan only for a three-year period and set an actual endpoint of the plan. You may consider this to be a pilot project after which you will decide whether or not to continue with the plan. This is probably the least likely option for strategic planning. It may be

better used for other types of projects such as implementing a new
reading program.

The third option is, in all probability, the most likely choice
for an evaluation of the strategic planning process for schools.
This option will provide a standard pattern for which to collect
and review data on a regular basis. It seems to fit best with most
schools because the efforts are typically ongoing and do not
have a definite end where school improvement is concerned. The
quarterly and year-end results can be compared from one year to
the next.

The formative evaluation can guide your team through the
revisions that may need to take place as a result of your findings.
To conduct the formative evaluation, gather the monitoring data at
each of the quarterly reviews. Using an internal approach, which is
conducted in-house most generally by members of the SPT, collect
the data from all areas and share the information at a meeting of
the SPT. Another method, which is preferred, is to bring in various
staff responsible for each of the goals and have them present the
data to the SPT. This approach is recommended because questions
can be asked of the members responsible for implementation. The
SPT could hold three different sessions, one for each goal, in order
to bring in a representative group of staff members responsible for
the implementation of the goals.

The data collection and reporting procedures you established
will enable you to create a standard format for presenting the data.
Each quarter, the same format should be followed when reporting
the data so that everyone knows what to expect. You will be able
to easily identify improvements made or areas of concern. Over
time, trends may begin to appear in the data that will assist to
inform your decision making.

A critical part of the process will be to review each step on
its own merits and decide if it should be continued, modified, or
eliminated. Evaluation is the tool that you and the SPT will use to
make judgments about the strategies that have been implemented.
There will, no doubt, be cases where determining which strategies
have been the most effective among those being implemented in
one particular goal area will be difficult. This is where qualitative
data will be useful. Anecdotal records or survey items, for example,
can provide insight in areas where determining which particular

action step within a strategy was the one to produce the results or if it could have been a combination of several action steps together. This is a point where bringing in staff members responsible for implementation can be useful as well.

You may decide that it is not necessary to utilize evaluation methods to assess the progress, and therefore, you will make use of the monitoring activities instead. You and the SPT will decide the exact methods and procedures to use. Be sure to develop and decide the methods prior to or very early in the implementation of the strategic plan. Everyone needs to know the exact data they will be expected to report. The following figure summarizes helpful tips for evaluation.

Tips for Evaluating the Plan

- There is no best way to conduct the evaluation.
- Use the evaluation methods that work best for your situation.
- Plan evaluation methods prior to or early in the implementation of the plan.
- Make use of both quantitative and qualitative data.

Gathering the Data for Monitoring and Evaluating the Plan

By this point in the process, you know what you want to achieve and you possess a good understanding of the data needed to illustrate your results. You will need to develop processes that will streamline your data gathering and reporting efforts. Enlist the help of technologically savvy staff members for this purpose. It is best to develop the data-gathering processes prior to the implementation of the strategic plan or early in the implementation phase. People within the organization who are working the plan need to know what data are to be gathered and how it will be presented. Each time data are gathered, monthly or quarterly, for instance, the data should be presented in the same fashion and format for ease of comparison. Develop forms or specific instruments on which to collect the required information and designate a person or team to be responsible for maintaining and storing the data. Once again, it is important to note that data gathering must be as simple as possible. You do not want to burden yourself and others with loads of paperwork that detract from carrying out the process itself. The more the reporting can be streamlined, the better.

For each of the action steps in your plan, you previously set an evaluation measure or an indicator of success on which to base judgments regarding the progress achieved. You need to gather as much relevant data as possible in order to facilitate the evidence-based or data-driven decision making. Evidence-based decision making operates on the premise that future decisions made by you and your SPT will be determined by the extent to which your school has or has not met the measures as stated within your overall goals. Focus on making changes only when the evidence or data dictate. Individual teachers must analyze their own data based on the classroom action plans.

Your data gathering and analysis should consist of both quantitative and qualitative data. As discussed in chapter 4, quantitative data are those data that are expressed numerically and are gathered from sources, such as test scores, the number of correct responses on a given item, or attendance counts. Quantitative data can be displayed visually in graphs, charts, and the like. Qualitative data are those which describe items in terms of a category or quality and are derived from sources, such as surveys, focus groups, and interviews. Qualitative data can also be displayed visually. For example, survey results can be compiled and a graph or bar chart can be used to display the number of responses in each category of a survey.

Status Reports

Gathering data to monitor and evaluate individual student progress can be accomplished through the use of status reports. A status report records detailed student information in a spreadsheet format that is reviewed monthly or quarterly by teachers. The status report is especially effective in schools where teachers share students. For example, if your school is set up in teams, a math teacher and a language arts teacher may share the same group of students during different periods of the day. The two teachers will work together on one status report for the group. General demographic information is listed first, such as name, parent name, and telephone number. Next, past test or assessment scores and grade information are listed. Then, any other relevant data are noted, such as IEP, LEP, or tutoring programs. Finally, general comments about the students' engagement, effort, or challenges are included. The purpose of the status report is to ensure that teachers are monitoring each student's progress on a regular basis. In addition, it identifies students' needs which can be addressed through the strategies in the action plans.

There are a number of web-based documents where you can house information such as the status report. You must make certain the documents are secure and are password protected to ensure the safety and confidentiality of the student information. By utilizing a web-based document, teachers can frequently update the document as new information is gathered. Teachers and administrators can view the most up-to-date information at any time.

Status Report

Teacher Names							Quarter/Year				
Student Name	Parent Name	Phone	Age/DOB	Read. Test Scores '12 '13	Math Test Scores '12 '13	Program (IEP, LEP)	Engagement (enter 1-5 for level of engagement) Eng.	Math	Sci.	Soc.St.	Comments

Figure 7.2. Status Report example

Chapter Summary

Data needed for monitoring and evaluation should be clearly established in the plan. Find ways to gather and report data as easily as possible. The same format should be used each time data are gathered for ease of comparison.

Monitoring strategies should be built into the plan so everyone knows the expectations. Monitoring can identify problem areas with the delivery of instruction and implementation of the action steps. Performed throughout the implementation of the plan, monitoring informs decision making during the process. Monitoring is an ongoing collection of information and review of the information collected. Monitoring also conveys the importance of the plan, inspires continued improvement, ensures results are being met, enables adjustments to be made along the way, and provides critical information for the evaluation process.

Evaluation strategies should likewise be built into the plan. Evaluation generally will take place at the end of a school year or at the end of the implementation of the plan. It is a review of progress and outcomes which examines long-term results. Evaluation can identify if and how the plan was successful and can examine how well the process worked. Evaluation determines whether or not your strategies were successful, identifies whether or not the goals were appropriate, documents results, provides comparison data, presents a true picture of the school, and delivers accountability.

In order for teachers to maintain a complete, up-to-date understanding of their students' skills and levels of performance, status reports should be used. Status reports will track important information needed to assess individual student progress. Status reports should be reviewed monthly or quarterly by teachers.

CHAPTER 8

Revising the Plan

Successful strategic plans are intended to be dynamic documents, indicating that they are meant to be revised as needed. There may be times, however, that few, if any, revisions will be necessary. For these reasons, this phase of the strategic planning process is possibly the most subjective and unique. No two schools will follow the same pattern for making revisions to their strategic plans. The revision phase will focus on the data gathered, as well as the professional judgment and discretion of the SPT, as you work to shape the changes. The revision process offers you the opportunity to refresh, upgrade, improve, or revitalize your strategic plan when indications are that results are not being met or that the plan is not proceeding as scheduled, for example. There is no right or wrong method for deciding what should be revised, if anything. Much of what you decide to do in this phase is dependent upon the type of monitoring and evaluating activities you have conducted and the progress you have made.

Periodic assessments that are conducted by means of the monitoring and evaluating activities provide you and the SPT with important information about the strategies and action steps that were originally developed in the planning stages. The hurdle now is how to determine whether or not a strategy or action step should be maintained, modified, or discontinued and replaced with a different strategy. Modifications made to the plan generally occur for one of three reasons:

- changes in the external environment
- changes in "client" needs
- perceived ineffectiveness of the current plan

External environment changes could be associated with, for example, federal or state mandates or guidelines that have changed. Alignment with the new mandates is needed in order to best prepare students for required assessments. If your state has recently added new types of questions, such as constructed response questions, to the state assessment, new strategies will be needed to ensure students are prepared for this type of question. Prior to the assessment, similar questions should be provided for practice.

"Client" needs could be related to the learning needs of the students. Perhaps there has been an influx of limited English-speaking students to the building. It will be necessary to add specific strategies to the plan to address the needs of this population.

A perceived ineffectiveness of the current plan may exist, for instance, after state assessment results are received at the end of the first year of implementation of the strategic plan. Results may not be as high as expected; therefore, you and the SPT conclude that change is needed. Teachers may report that they are finding a certain strategy to be ineffective. Further investigation through qualitative data gathering and analysis may confirm the report; thus, you conclude that revision is necessary.

What is the proper time to abandon elements of the original plan and start fresh? Rest assured, you should never throw out the entire plan and begin anew. This is a good time to think back to the planning stages when a great deal of time and effort were spent creating then refining the strategies and the action steps. You and the SPT instituted what you determined to be the most effective plan for your building as you collectively selected the research based strategies to implement. However, keep in mind

SCHOOL IMPROVEMENT: REVITALIZE YOUR SCHOOL WITH STRATEGIC PLANNING 139

that successful strategic plans are meant to be flexible and fluid documents. Even the most carefully written plans may not produce the desired results; consequently, some revision may be necessary. The revision process will typically involve a minor fine-tuning of the current plan or altering the action steps within the strategies rather than an extensive overhaul of the plan. Any changes that are made should be based on solid evidence from your monitoring and evaluating processes. Do not be tempted or let yourself be swayed to change the plan without sufficient implementation time or without solid evidence of the need to change.

Revising the plan should include an examination of step 1 and step 2 of the planning process. Briefly review the purpose, mission, vision, and goals to ensure that the upcoming changes are aligned. Reevaluate all of the data, from the initial data collected to the most current data collected. Make certain that any new strategies written into the plan are aligned with this information. If the evaluation shows that sufficient progress toward the goals is not being made and that anticipated results are not being achieved, you then can determine that changes need to occur based on the these results. At this point, it is time to convene the SPT to discuss the modifications that need to be prepared. Changes may need to take place in the implementation of the strategies and action steps, the strategies and action steps themselves, or in both. Whatever the case, communication and support are necessary in this phase. Once the revisions have been made, you will proceed on to step 4 of the process, implementing the plan, and from there continue on with step 5, monitoring and evaluating the plan, then again to step 6, revising the plan.

Changes in the Strategies and Action Steps

Should you find that results are not being met due to the strategies and action steps themselves, the SPT will need to meet to revise the plan. Once more, meet with teachers in the content area of concern to gather information on the perceived problems in order to determine the best possible solutions.

As changes occur in education, whether they are changes in state assessments or perhaps changes in your district curricula, holding on to your original goals is sometimes unproductive. You will find that there may be times when the strategies and action steps you originally included in your plan just don't work or simply do not meet the needs as you had anticipated. The best thing you can do at this point is to openly examine the concerns. Look at your school with a thoughtful eye. By coming together as a team, you will be able to collaboratively discuss the issues, and with the data gathered through the monitoring and evaluation processes, identify that some aspects of the plan did not bring about the desired results. You must be ready to make changes to the degree the situation requires. In some cases, a fine-tuning of the strategies is all that is needed. In other cases, more extensive change is necessary. When you decide to make revisions to your plan, work with the teachers in the specific content area in question to obtain an accurate understanding of the situation. The team must be open to investigating new strategies that may be a better match for the current condition. Once the changes have been decided upon, meet again with those teachers to ensure they understand their responsibilities in terms of implementing the new or revised strategies and for revising their classroom action plans. The person or team charged with maintaining and storing the data for the strategic plan should also be responsible for tracking any changes and revisions that have been made. Concentrate on these actions as you make revisions to your plan.

- Principal, SPT leaders, and department heads or team leaders should review the current strategies and action steps.
- Review the monitoring data that have been gathered.
- Discuss progress that has been made using the current strategies and action steps.
- Identify areas needing revisions.
- Consult with teachers who are affected by the proposed revisions.
- Decide upon revisions to be made.
- Review the teachers' revised classroom action plans.
- Ensure that teachers understand and are able to implement the revisions.
- Track any changes or revisions to the plan.

Changes in the Implementation of Strategies and Action Steps

After much review and consideration, suppose you conclude that the strategies you have in place are appropriate. What you discover, however, is that there remains an issue with the implementation of the strategies. During the implementation of the strategic plan, observations were carried out with the teachers responsible for executing the strategies. As problems were observed, support and assistance were provided. Many of these issues were addressed during the implementation of the plan. Should you find that the intended results are still not being met upon review and the problem is with the implementation of the strategies or action steps, you will proceed in a different manner. Monitoring and data collection are extremely important in this case to pinpoint the deficiencies. You may find that teachers are not implementing the action steps completely or correctly. Typically, problems with the implementation of the plan will occur for one of these three reasons:

1. The teacher does not have a good understanding or knowledge of the strategies to be implemented or perhaps even the subject matter itself.
2. The teacher lacks the skill necessary to present the strategies to his or her students.
3. The teacher's attitude toward either the strategies or the entire process is standing in the way of his or her ability to implement the plan.

At this point, additional measures should be taken to assist the teachers with proper implementation which can be handled in a number of ways. Making certain that implementation is consistently accomplished is best handled in an applied manner. In other words, guide the teachers with the use of modeling or demonstration. A teacher who is successfully implementing the strategies and who has generated desired results can be a valuable resource. Other strategies may be used that are agreed upon by the administration and the teachers involved. Keep in mind that this could be a very delicate situation to handle. The manner in which you approach the assistance is very important to the outcome. The assistance should be as supportive as possible and should not be viewed as evaluative or critical with regard to teachers not producing the desired gains. The purpose of the assistance for teachers is to improve their ability to implement the strategies as desired in order to achieve the best possible results with their students.

Nonetheless, you are at this stage of the process and find that obstacles still exist with the manner in which certain teachers are executing the plan. These are instances where further intervention is needed. Generally speaking, in this case, additional professional development or training is necessary for the teachers who are not implementing the strategies as written and, consequently, are not making the expected gains with their students.

As the principal, you will have the greatest knowledge of identifying where the difficulties lie. Should you have other administrators conducting observations, as well, meet together and identify teachers who are in need of further guidance. Identify the teachers then pinpoint the areas of concern. Plan sessions to assist the teachers in becoming proficient in implementing the strategies. Provide opportunities for teachers to discuss and share implementation methods with one another or pair teachers together to support good implementation practices. Professional development time during team, department, or staff meetings can be set aside for these activities. Outside resources such as workshops or seminars may be necessary. Consider creating a performance improvement plan for these teachers to delineate the exact steps that should be taken for them to improve. Follow these suggestions for providing guidance to teachers in need of assistance with the implementation of the strategic plan action steps:

- Identify problem areas through the monitoring activities.
- In department or team meetings, provide reflection time for teachers to discuss ideas and share practices that are producing results.
- Provide one-on-one assistance.
- Model proper implementation of the strategies.
- Pair teachers to work together on strategies.
- Make use of outside resources, if necessary.
- Initiate a performance improvement plan.

Referring back to the monitoring and evaluation phase of the process, conducting a formative evaluation at the end of each year of the plan is the suggested method. After the year-end evaluation is performed, the SPT should then be prepared to craft revisions to the plan based on the findings of the evaluation. Keeping in mind that this is a continuous process, the evaluation signals the end of one year, nevertheless it also signifies the beginning of a new year. Analyzing progress may be the end of one cycle, but the information gleaned from that analysis is the starting point for the next planning cycle. All of the information gathered during the evaluation process should be analyzed for inclusion in the next strategic plan update.

The goals that were originally identified include benchmarks for the end of the first, second, and third years. We have already discussed what to do if results fall below the expected target, but what should happen if results are higher than expected? That is an excellent problem to encounter, but should it occur, have a plan in mind. Perhaps the original goals that were set were too low or this was a particularly good year. Regardless of the reason, reassess the targets that were originally set in the plan and determine if the targets for the second and third years should be increased.

The strategic plan must be mission driven and results oriented. To conduct a comprehensive review for the purpose of revising the plan, the SPT should examine the mission and vision statements and determine whether each is still valid. Typically, the statements will remain relatively the same but minor adjustments may be warranted. If no issues are identified, they can remain the same. The point is to make certain that the statements continue to be current and relevant. A review at the end of each year will ensure that the specific, results-oriented strategies are based on the mission.

Any revisions made to the strategic plan must be documented and tracked. If a strategy has been removed from the plan, for example, you do not want to add that strategy back to the plan at a later date, not realizing that it has already been attempted and removed. You need to know what worked as well as what didn't work. A systematic method should be employed for tracking changes and revisions made to the plan.

Thinking back to the concept of the parking lot list discussed in chapter 2, this is the time to review the list and discuss whether or not any of the items from the list should be incorporated into the plan. New goals should not be introduced; however, new strategies could be included that may come from the parking list.

Chapter Summary

The extent to which revisions to your strategic plan will be made is dependent on the results achieved. The evaluation results will be used to identify the areas that should be considered for revision. Adjustments may be necessary due to changes in the external environment, changes in client needs, or perceived ineffectiveness of the current plan.

Two distinct areas exist for consideration of possible changes. Changes may be needed in the strategies and action steps themselves or in the implementation of the strategies and action steps. In either case, problem areas should be identified then discussed with the teachers. Determine where revisions are going to be made and make certain everyone is aware of the changes and understands them. The SPT should be responsible for updating the revisions to the strategic plan. Once the revisions are complete, teachers can then revise their classroom action plans. The SPT or another individual or group should be responsible for tracking the changes that have been made to the plan.

In the process of revising the plan, the mission and vision statements should be examined to ensure they remain relevant. In addition, by revisiting these elements, you will keep them in mind when considering revisions. While changes most likely will not be made, the statements should, nevertheless, be reviewed.

Helping teachers improve can be a difficult situation which should be handled with care. If interventions have been implemented and problems still remain, it may be necessary to initiate a teacher improvement plan or involve outside resources to assist.

CONCLUSION

This book was written with the building principal in mind. It is the building principal who is vitally important to school success and can influence and impact an entire school building from top to bottom. The building principal must first have the belief in himself or herself that his or her leadership can impact student learning and achievement. From there, he or she must possess the leadership skills to create a vision, maintain high expectations for reaching that vision, and be able to lead the staff in this endeavor. It takes collaboration and communication to build a strong staff that supports the vision. Finally, a commitment by every member of the organization is necessary to bring about the desired changes. Once these essential elements are in place, you will have the foundation for building school improvement through strategic planning.

Strategic planning is an absolute must for schools. If your school or district already has a school improvement plan that has been completed for state or federal requirements, the school, nevertheless, needs a process that will specifically reach the level of each and every student. For it is when individual student levels of performance are monitored and individual needs of each student are addressed that progress will be made. Most plans that have been created to meet requirements are written in generalities that indicate what teachers and staff should be doing. The model presented in this book is a student-centered plan rather than an adult-centered plan which is the key element of the process presented. It is vitally important to determine where students are and move them forward. A school hoping to improve cannot write a general plan just to satisfy a requirement but must view the plan as a living, working document that is applied on a daily basis. A building plan will not produce the kind of results you want until the plan encompasses student levels of achievement and monitoring of student progress from top to bottom.

Much has been written about reforming, restructuring, and transforming schools. But year after year, decade after decade, educators find themselves in the same position and ask the same question: how can we increase the academic achievement for all students? Although improvement plans have been a requirement for a number of years, achievement is not increasing as desired. A great amount of time and effort seems to be spent on producing the plan and, in many cases, meeting deadlines for submitting the plan, but less effort is expended on working the plan and on holding everyone accountable for outcomes. When efforts are placed on the later, results will begin to show.

I refer to using the process presented and discussed throughout this book as revitalizing the school. You already have all of the elements you need to make the improvements that are necessary for student success. Now you must be the catalyst for influencing and revitalizing the staff to make it happen. Strategic planning can be the means for making the kind of improvement any school would aspire to by following through with this specific, structured plan. Through the systematic and consistent application of the steps presented, you can achieve the results you want. It does not take a new program to make a difference. School improvement can be achieved with the desire, determination, and drive to put this process in motion and implement the steps as described.

All the best to you in your endeavor to improve student academic achievement and to make a difference in the lives of your students.

INDEX

REFERENCES

All About Strategic Planning. www.managementhelp.org. Retrieved 2/14/2012.

Business Planning: Developing a Strategic Plan. www.planware. org. Retrieved 4/2/2012.

Cotton, K., (2003). *Principals and Student Achievement: What the Research Says*. Alexandria, VA: Association for Supervision and Curriculum Development.

Covey, S. (1994). *First Things First*. New York, NY. Free Press.

DuFour, R., Eaker, R., (1998). *Professional Learning Communities at Word: Best Practices for Enhancing Student Achievement*. Bloomington, IN: National Educational Service.

Educational Leadership Informative Assessment: Making Strategic Planning Work. www.ascd.org. Retrieved 3/2/2011.

Kotter, J.P. (1996). *Leading Change*. Boston, MA: Harvard Business School Press.

Kotter, J.P. (2007, January). Leading change: why transformation efforts fail. *Harvard Business Review*, 85(1), 96-103.

Lazarus, B.D. (1993). Guided notes: Effects with secondary and postsecondary students with mild disabilities. *Education and Treatment of Children*, 16, 272-289.

Martinko, M. (1995). *Attribution Theory: An Organizational Perspective*, Delray Beach, FL: St. Lucie Press.

Marzano, R.J., Pickering, D.J., & Pollock, J.E. (2001). *Classroom instruction that works: Research-based strategies for increasing student achievement.* Alexandria, VA: Association for Supervision and Curriculum Development.

Murdock-Miller, P., (1988). *Powerful Leadership Skills for Women.* Shawnee Mission, KS: National Seminars Publications.

Reeves, D.B. (2006). *The learning leader: How to focus school improvement for better results.* Alexandria, VA: Association for Supervision and Curriculum Development.

Rosenthal, R., Jacobson, L. (1992). *Pygmalion in the Classroom,* Irvington, NJ: Irvington Publishing.

Strategic Planning Failure. www.referenceforbusiness.com. Retrieved 11/12/2011.

Schlechty, P.C. (1997). *Inventing better schools: An action plan for educational reform.* San Francisco, CA: Jossey-Bass.

Schmoker, M. (2004, February). Tipping point: From reckless reform to substantive instructional improvement. *Phi Delta Kappan,* 85(6), 424-432.

Wiley, J. (2006). Creating and Implementing Your Strategic Plan, San Francisco, CA: Jossey-Bass.

CPSIA information can be obtained
at www.ICGtesting.com
Printed in the USA
LVOW11s1601151017
552519LV00002B/156/P